Y0-EDW-184

Discovery of a Genius

William Dean Howells and Henry James

DISCOVERY OF A GENIUS

William Dean Howells and Henry James

Compiled and Edited by

ALBERT MORDELL

Introduction by

SYLVIA E. BOWMAN

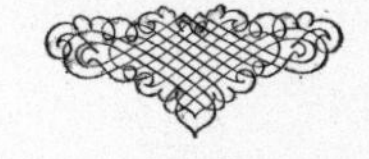

TWAYNE PUBLISHERS • NEW YORK

Library of Congress Catalog No. 61-9852
Manufactured in the United States by
CAPITAL CITY PRESS • MONTPELIER • VERMONT

CONTENTS

PREFACE

Discovery of a Genius is the first collection of the published articles and book reviews written by William Dean Howells about Henry James's publications. Except for an article—"Daisy Miller," and a small piece on James in *My Literary Passions,*—reprinted by Howells and for two articles included in other anthologies,[1] these critical estimates have remained buried in the periodicals in which they first appeared.

The articles and reviews of Howells are important; for they indicate that he was one of James's "first, warmest, truest" and most consistent admirers and that he, because of his editorial positions, had rendered James great service by encouraging him, by publishing his fiction, by calling attention to it, and by interpreting or defending it. Because of the revived interest today in the life and fiction of Howells, these collected items are of interest for they portray him as the critic who early recognized the genius of James.

James recognized his indebtedness to Howells when he wrote him from London on February 19, 1912, in recognition of his benefactor's seventy-fifth birthday:

> "My debt to you began well-nigh half a century ago, in the most personal way possible, and then kept growing with your own admirable growth—but always rooted in the early intimate benefit. The benefit was that you held out your open editorial hand to me at the time I began to write—and I allude especially to the summer of 1866—

> with a frankness and sweetness of hospitality that was really the making of me, the making of the confidence that required help and sympathy and that I should otherwise, I think, have strayed and stumbled about a long time without acquiring. You showed me the way and opened me the door; you wrote to me, and confessed yourself struck with me—I have never forgotten the beautiful thrill of *that*. You published me at once—and paid me, above all, with a dazzling promptitude; magnificently, I felt, and so that nothing since has ever quite come up to it. More than this even, you cheered me on with a sympathy that was in itself an inspiration. I mean that you talked to me and listened to me—ever so patiently and genially, and suggestively conversed and consorted with me. This won me to you irresistibly and made you the most interesting person I knew—lost as I was in the charming sense that my best friend was an editor, and an almost insatiable editor, and that such a delicious being as that was a kind of property of my own."[2]

Howells was able to help "open the door" for James because of his connections with important periodicals.[3] Before he resigned in 1881 from the *Atlantic Monthly*, Howells had not only urged J. T. Fields to continue to publish James's fiction but had written reviews of *The Passionate Pilgrim and Other Tales*, *Transatlantic Sketches*,[4] *French Poets and Novelists*, *Hawthorne*, and *Daisy Miller*. In 1882 he also wrote an article "Henry James, Jr." for the *Century*.

While Howells conducted the "Editor's Study" in *Harper's Monthly* from January, 1886, to March, 1892, he wrote words of approbation about the novels and tales of James which were not so popular as some of his other, earlier ones: *The Princess Casamassima*, *The Reverberator*, *A London Life*, and *The Tragic Muse*. In 1895, Howells was writing for *Harper's Weekly*; and he wrote—interestingly enough, as we shall see—a favorable review of *Terminations* in the same issue in which he praised George Moore's *Celibates.* While he conducted the "Easy Chair" in *Harper's Monthly* from December, 1900, until his death in 1920, he wrote for it in 1901 at least one notice about a book by James, *The Soft Side*; in 1902, a defense of *Daisy Miller*, for *Harper's Bazaar*; and, in 1903, an article assessing quite accurately James's fiction for the *North American Review.*

Although Howells was one of the first to perceive James's importance as a writer, he was often attacked as a critic. For example, Lafcadio Hearn stated that Howells' "power of criticism was limited to Sunday-School standards,—good and respectable standards in their way, but never intended for the measurement of centuries and civilizations."[5] Although Professor Lyon Phelps considered Howells to be a good novelist, he also thought him a poor critic. Oscar Firkins in *William Dean Howells* (1924) stated, however, that Howells "brought to the craft of reviewing a catholicity of reception and a humanity of procedure which conducted to its renovation and to his own honor"; and he observed—after ignoring the reviews of James's fiction in the *Atlantic Monthly*—that Howells' reviews in the *North American*, including the one about James, "contain not a few of his weightiest and most striking declarations."

To Firkins, the style of the reviews written for the *Atlantic Monthly* was attractive but unsure; but the articles published in the "Editor's Study" in *Harper's Monthly* had a felicity that was unerring and unceasing and a definite charm when the personality of the writer peered through the impersonal style. What made Howells a great critic, wrote Firkins as he considered *Criticism and Fiction* (1891) which contained many of these articles, was his voicing "with power and authority the principle to which the fiction of the future may look for its standard and inspiration."[6]

Although no one can contest the inspiration and the importance of *Criticism and Fiction* in the annals of American realism, we must admit that Howells in the hundreds of reviews which lie buried in the files of the *Atlantic Monthly* and of *Harper's Monthly* showed that he was only too often inclined to praise a book. The story is related that he once told a reviewer that, if he found a book bad, he should say a good word about the typography or binding. Despite his desire to be generous, Howells could pounce upon a writer—and often did; and he could also, when attacked, be not only aggressive but abusive.

Although Howells erred in his assessments of some writers, his praise of Ralph Keeler (the model for Fulkerson in *A Hazard of New Fortunes*), John W. De Forest, Twain, James, Norris, Bellamy, and Crane attests to his merit as a critic. Although we may forgive his errors of judgment if we remember Emerson's of Poe, James's of Thoreau, Lowell's of Whitman, and Mark Twain's of Cooper, we must also note Howells' critical inconsistencies and his biases. Although he could praise Norris' *McTeague* and Crane's *Maggie* and although he eulogized Emile Zola, he could not approve of Dreiser's *Sister Carrie.* Howells admired in Zola the spirit which aroused pity and desired justice; and he asserted that, if Zola depicted "indecency," he did so to unveil the evils it produced. Yet Dreiser was adamantly opposed to social injustice; he disliked business intrigue; and his portrayal of Hurstwood was intended to arouse pity.

Howells sought truth of portraiture or fidelity to life as a result of his early reading of the comedies of Carlo Goldoni,[7] and he was, therefore, highly critical of romanticism and of historical novels. He limited his realism to exclude vulgarity of expression; portrayals of unusual events which would not meet the approval of the "genteel" or puritanical woman or which were "vicious panderings to passion." In his lecture "Novel Writing and Novel Reading" of 1899,[8] Howells asserted that the dramatic situation was obsolete, called resorting to it an old superstition, and demanded that the novelist endeavor to give exactly the effects of life—though he admitted that he, having been reared in a "false school," had never been able to do so. Although Howells stated that the "coming novelist" would feel the beauty of truth, he did not realize that, by depicting only the commonplace events and omitting the sordid ones which *do* comprise a percentage of life's experiences, he was arguing for the depiction of only the dull, unimportant events which readers would tolerate only if the portrayal were accompanied by a magic style, vital ideas, or noble morals. Indeed, a chapter about a husband who felt tired at work, came home, and took a nap would not be half so interesting as the story of the husband who came home to find his wife entertaining a lover—as was the case in *Vanity Fair* by Thackeray, an author Howells unjustly disliked.

Although Howells did not always dwell on "the smiling aspects of life"—a phrase repeated too frequently by his hostile critics—he could appreciate writers (as we have noted) who dwelt on the stormy and tragic aspects of life and who became matryrs for liberty—and the latter is to be noticed in his book *Modern Italian Poets* (1887). Edwin H. Cady deems this book to be Howells' worst, but Woodress in *Howells and Italy* thinks more highly of it after analyzing it. Although the book had been begun twenty years before it was published in 1887 and the contents had been used for lectures which James listened to with rapture, *Modern Italian Poets* never had a wide appeal; for it was concerned with twenty poets who, with the exceptions of Leopardi, Manzoni, and Alfieri, were unknown to the English reading world.

In this book Howells showed some insight about and sympathy for militant liberalism. He was charmed with the efforts of the poets in behalf of liberty, and he agreed with their anti-clericalism. Furthermore, even the pessimistic Leopardi appealed to him—as he appealed to Gladstone, to James Thomson, and to Georg Brandes, who wrote a preface to the German translation of his works.

When we turn to the criticisms which Howells made of James's fiction, it is interesting to compare them with the twelve[9] he made of Mark Twain's which he collected in *My Mark Twain: Reminiscences and Criticisms* (1910). Of his earlier criticisms of Twain, which were published in the same magazines as those about James, Howells wrote that they were stiff, pedantic and patronizing; but he considered his later ones of Twain to be suppler, wiser, more diffident—and his judgment of these could also be applied to all those he wrote about James. The reviews of James's fiction are superior to those about Twain; and the reason lies perhaps in the greater intellectual, literary, and technical affinity of Howells with James than with Twain.

When we consider the differences and likenesses of James and Howells, we find that they appear—as Everett Carter noted in *Howells and the Age of Realism*[10]—in their subject matter, their attitudes toward life, their ethical aim in fiction, their techniques. Both James and Howells belonged to the school of realists who desired to base their fiction upon contemporaneous life and to represent it. To do so, they both believed that life had to be transformed by art to give it form and effect—to make the novel seem like life. Though both men were realists, they were also "limited realists"; for both Howells and James skirted around the aspects of life and love which the naturalists were to treat with such gusto—and with such disdain for both James and Howells. Though both Howells and James believed in the realism of the commonplace, James's characters were far from common; they were—because of the view of life and the intent of James—uncommonly sensitive, intelligent, reacting individuals.

James and Howells were also alike in their view of Americans; they pictured them in their novels as being the moral superiors of the amoral Europeans. Howells, although he also wrote the international type of novel which James was to make so famous, was, however, to become more and more preoccupied with the American scene, its problem, and its panaceas. Unlike James who wrote only one political novel,[11] Howells was to write many of social criticism and, under the influence of Edward Bellamy, two Utopian novels.

Both men were also agreed that "the simple ethic" which motivated their writing was to show the importance of renunciation of selfishness; for if a man maintained his selfishness, he dwelt in the dark dungeon of self and denied himself the opportunity of growing through giving of himself to others. As Carter has pointed out, both writers were essentially pragmatic in their ethical attitudes; for they accepted that "which worked as right," rejected other standards of right and wrong, and abstained from moral preachments.

Both men differed, however, in their basic concept of life. To Howells and to Twain, during most of their careers, the determining factor of the end results of a man's life depended upon his rational or irrational approach. If man were ruled by passions or irrationality, he would be doomed to discomfort and misery; if he were rational and if he used his common sense, his reward would be comfort and fulfillment. Furthermore, both Twain and Howells presented the realities of life—and they tested ideas as they appeared in action (as, for example, the famous test of ideas about friendship and the demands of slavery in *Huckleberry Finn.*)

To James, however, the surface realities were deceptive; as he peered below them, he perceived that men and women were filled with renunciations, repressions, conflicts, and even ideals which made life tragic but often noble. To James, the test of an ideal or of a situation was its mental effect; and he thought that through their intellectual experiences men truly lived—

suffer though they might—and developed. For this reason, James chose his uncommon characters—people who, like the characters of George Eliot and Turgenev[12], could be placed in a situation drawn from a "germ"—an anecdote—and with their sensibilities and their ideals face the test, perceive, suffer, grow, and, as a rule, make a noble renunciation.

Because of their attitudes toward life and because of their differences of intents, Howells' and James's techniques eventually differed greatly. Though both believed in dramatic presentation of life, James turned from the materialism and values of his era and, instead of attempting to reform it as Howells ultimately did, tried to indicate that the salvation of the individual lay in his own mind—and showed that his own lay in art. Because of his interest in the inner life, in art forms, and aesthetic values, James developed his involved method and style of presentation which Howells called a "synthesis" and which won James such critical acclaim later for the *Wings of the Dove, The Ambassadors,* and *The Golden Bowl.* Though Howells used the dramatic presentation as a means of establishing rapport with the reader and of obtaining verisimilitude, this method was only one of the many he employed in his loosely constructed novels. Furthermore, Howells, who strove for clarity, detested obscurity and ambiguity—and yet, despite these characteristics of James's fiction, Howells never ceased to appreciate his work or to defend it. In Howells' continued appreciation of James's fiction we can remark not only his loyalty to a friend but—more important as we consider Howells as a critic—his catholicity of appreciation; his generous, flexible judgment; and his looking backward to an earlier James while he looked forward to his eventual recognition.

Howells' attempt to appreciate the changed method of James's *The Portrait of a Lady* and of *Wings of the Dove* is shown in two of the three longer articles which he wrote. In "Henry James, Jr." which was published in *The Century* of

November, 1882, Howells expressed his lingering appreciation for such stories as "Poor Richard" and "A Passionate Pilgrim." In connection with them, he noted his liking for James's "whole clear and beautiful style," his poetic qualities, and the dramatic scenes of "A Passionate Pilgrim." Howells stated that he regretted James's loss of poetry but admitted that no one had the right "to ask a man to keep on being a poet."

As he looked back at the earlier work of James where "he stood at the dividing ways of the novel and the romance," Howells stated that he was sorry that James "declared even superficially for the former" for "his best efforts seem to me those of romance"—and yet he was intrigued by the characters of his later work.

In his remarks about *The Portrait of a Lady,* Howells stated that he found in it not "much of that I should call dramatic" but "an amount of analysis which I should call superabundance if it were not all such good literature." After remarking that the main business of the novelist was "to possess his reader with a due conception of his characters and the situations in which they find themselves," Howells stated that "if he does more or less than this he equally fails" and that he had "sometimes thought that Mr. James's danger was to do more." He then admitted, however, that he had, because of his own enjoyment, hesitated to be critical of this "rather narrow, technical" matter.

When he discussed James's analysis of motives, he compared him to George Eliot but then remarked that with Eliot an ethical purpose was dominant and with James the artistic. In comparing the heroines of the two authors, he pointed out that Eliot's Dorothea aroused sympathy for "grand aims that chiefly concern others" and that James's Isabel Archer created it for "beautiful dreams that primarily concern herself". Both were "the most nobly intentioned women in modern fiction"; but Isabel was "the more subtly divined of the two."

After speaking of James's international fiction and of his characterizations—for Howells liked "better to speak of his people than of the conduct of his novels"—Howells reintroduced the subject of James's greater interest in the character of his people than in their fate; for "when he has fully developed their character he leaves them to what destiny the reader pleases." Although Howells had said that this trait—as well as a tendency to confuse the reader because of objectivity and reserve of presentation—was one which had to be conceded to James, Howells then speculated as to whether or not the readers would accept a "novel which is an analysis and not a story, which is apt to leave him arbiter of the destiny of the author's creations." Although James gratified the philosophic desires of the reader to learn what the "novelist thinks about persons and situations," James forbore "to tell . . . the last state of his people . . . because that" did not interest him. After stating that a "large-minded criticism" would "insist that it was childish to demand that it must interest him", Howells frankly declared that he was not sure that his "criticism" was "sufficiently large-minded for this"; for he liked "a finished story."

Howells ended his essay with a tribute to James as "an annalist, or analyst" who "fascinates us from his first page to his last". Earlier in the essay he had remarked that James was the exemplar of the school of fiction that had derived from Hawthorne, Eliot, and Daudet; but whether or not James would decide the nature of the novel remained to be seen.

In 1901 in "Mr. James's *Daisy Miller*" Howells developed the theme introduced in "Henry James, Jr." of the misunderstanding which the reader had of James's Daisy because of his method of presentation; but, despite the enmity of American women for his heroine, Howells announced that there was no writer who could vie with James in the creation of women. Although he forecasted that James would eventually "take that eminent place for which he has no rival" (for James was "this unique psychologist who deals artist-wise with his knowledge of human nature"), Howells in his essay evinced a desire that James would return "in the interest of history" to the contributions to "polite learning which his internationals are." Although Howells defended and explained Daisy because she was too frequently associated with the name of James, he could not resist comment about the earlier work of James; Howells recognized, however that in James's later work in which he turned to English life, he "has done better work, because maturer work, in the treatment of this alien material."

Of these three articles, the one which Howells wrote in 1903, "Mr. James's Later Work," for the *North American Review* is perhaps of greatest interest. Although he touched once again upon the enmity of women for James's superb female creations, he concentrated in this article upon *Wings of the Dove*, *The Awkward Age*, and *The Sacred Fount*. Despite Howells' interesting comments about these novels, we are more concerned with those about penetration of meaning in James's fiction and about obscurity—which, as already noted, Howells' disliked.

Of the discovery of meaning in James, Howells stated that he had "a theory that it is not well to penetrate every recess of an author's meaning. It robs him of the charm of mystery . . ." He then added, interestingly enough, that "the somewhat labyrinthine construction of Mr. James's later sentences lends itself to the practice of the self-denial necessary to the preservation of this charm. What I feel sure of is that he has a meaning in it all, and that by and by, perhaps when I least expect it, I shall surprise his meaning. In the meanwhile, I rest content with what I do know. In spite of all the Browning Clubs . . . all of Browning is not clear, but enough of Browning is clear for any real lover of his poetry." Later in the article Howells stated that the total effect of James's realism was such that "it does not matter . . . how the people talk,—or in what labyrinthine parentheses they let their unarriving language wander."

In discussing *The Awkward Age* and especially the loss of the general in the particular in James's fiction, Howells commented that what James "does is simply to show you these people mainly on the outside, as you mainly see people in the world, and to let you divine them and their ends from what they do and say. They are presented with infinite pains; as far as their appearance (though they are very little described) goes, you are not suffered to make a mistake. But he does not analyze them for you; rather he synthesizes them, and carefully hands them over to you in a sort of integrity very uncommon in the characters of fiction. One might infer from this that his method was dramatic, somewhat like Tourguenieff, say; but I do not know that his method is dramatic. I do not recall from the books more than one passage of dramatic intensity."

After complimenting James upon his mastery in these three books and after stating that he would leave the question of obscurity to those who might be more interested in the problem than he, Howells remarked that he was certain that the design was significant to James and that not finding it was the fault of the reader. Howells did, however, give advice about how to read James to the reader who sought enlightenment.

In the last part of this essay, Howells returned to his imagined female interlocutress to answer her questions about why readers should not "have studies of life which are not . . . conundrums." Howells replied by pointing out that life itself was a conundrum to which disciplined guessing might find the answer and that he himself preferred the author who kept him "guessing, with a pleasure, an edification, in the suggestive, instructive way he has of asking his conundrums . . . to the authors who do not tax my curiosity, who shove their answers at me before I have had a chance to try whether I cannot guess them." Howells then paid James tribute as a "great psychologist, who has the imagination of a poet, the wit of a keen humorist, the conscience of an impeccable moralist, the temperament of a philosopher, and the wisdom of a rarely experienced witness of the world. . . ."

From these essays we note that Howells lingered long over the earlier James; tried to explain his obscurity in terms still used in reference today to such writers as T. S. Eliot; had difficulty with James's unended stories and techniques; wondered about his analysis and his synthesis and missed dramatic intensity; but appreciated greatly his characters. These articles indicate that Howells found it difficult to accept the James of the later periods—but that he succeeded in doing so to such an extent that he could defend and even extol him.

Although Howells also never failed in his letters to praise James's fiction and to assure him, when he despaired because of his lack of sales, that he, not Howells, was the outstanding writer of the period upon whom all aspiring young writers focussed their attention, Howells and James often differed politely in their unpublished opinions of each others' work. Howells, after reading and accepting as an editor *The American*, wrote James as a reader-friend that he could not understand why his central characters, after having cleared the path for their marriage, had to renounce their happiness. James, on the other hand, when he had read *A Hazard of New Fortunes*, wrote an enthusiastic letter to Howells on May 17, 1890. In the midst of compliments about a novel whose theme would not appeal to him, James wrote that his objections to some features of the book had no "relevancy whatever as grounds of dislike—simply because you communicate so completely *what* you undertake to communicate." He also stated that "there's a whole quarter of the heaven upon which, in the matter of composition, you seem consciously—is it consciously—to have turned your back."

James expanded a little more fully upon his opinion of

Howells and of this novel in his letter to his brother William to whom he wrote that he noticed that Howells took no pains about style; that he did not care for the people who passed by Howells' window—his characters; and that all he saw in Howells was the power of communicability. This assessment of his fellow writer was not new; for as early as August of 1870, James in writing to Grace Norton about *Their Wedding Journey,* had stated that Howells had secondary or tertiary talents and worked off his slender, primitive capital. In August, 1871, James wrote to Charles Eliot Norton that Howells had little intellectual curiosity and compared him to a "poor man" holding a diamond and wondering how he could use it. James wrote, however, several favorable criticisms of Howells' work and he stated that he was a leader in realistic fiction; it must be admitted, however, that Howells seemed to have more admiration for James than James had for him.

It is also interesting to note the attitudes of Howells and James toward each other's critical work and toward different writers. In Howells' opinion of James's critical studies, we find the same generous, humble, complimentary one that he evinced about James's fiction. When Howells was writing many of the critical articles which he considered his best—for he later included them in *Criticism and Fiction*—he wrote on October 10, 1888, to James: "I want to tell you now that I think your *Partial Portraits* wonderfully good work. It makes all my critical work seem clumsy and uncouth."

Although James might speak lightly of his own critical work, as in the letter he sent to Robert Louis Stevensen in August of 1893 in which he called his *Essays in London and Elsewhere* "a volume of thin trifles" which did contain "some pretty writing—not addresses to the fishes," he did not pass over the blemishes in Howells' criticisms. On January 2, 1888, James wrote Howells quite frankly that he on occasions combined things that did not go together, that he sometimes made mistakes of proportion, and that he was inclined in general to insist more upon restrictions and limitations than upon other aspects of the work. Howells was, however, probably not too much affected by James's comments; for he included some of the criticized criticisms in *Criticism and Fiction*.

When we consider the reviews that Howells and James wrote about other authors, we find that both frequently discussed general literary topics such as realism, romanticism, analytical insight, techniques, and environment as the source and inspiration of literature. These subjects must also have occupied parts of their conversation during the early years of their friendship as James enthusiastically discussed French writers and Howells expounded upon Italian ones. It is also possible that just as James interested Howells in French literature, Howells' conversations about Hawthorne may have resulted in James's submitting—as Edel has suggested[13]—two romances in the Hawthorne vein, though this is not certain.

Aside from discussing James's *Gabrielle de Bergerac*, which Howells tells us James read aloud to him and his family before it was published serially in the *Atlantic* in the summer of 1867, the two men must have discussed Whitman's poetry. Howells had begun as an admirer of Whitman; and, before he had met the poet at Pfaff's in New York in August of 1860, he had commented upon his poetry in the Ohio *State Journal* and enthusiastically admired "Bardic Smybols" which had appeared in the *Atlantic* of April, 1860. He also wrote a review of the third edition of *Leaves of Grass* for the *Ashtabula Sentinel*; and this review, considered by Edwin H. Cady in *The Road to Realism* as "by far his best piece of literary criticism,"[14] was republished August 11, 1860, in the *Saturday Review*, the favorite publication of the Bohemians of Pfaff's. Howells' review indicated that he was in a fluctuating mood about Whitman; for, as Cady has pointed out,[15] Howells recognized

Whitman's power and beauty and right to be heard but disliked his revelation of the secrets of the body and his sexual references. All in all, Howells thought that Whitman had been "both overrated and underrated."

James from the first was hostile to Whitman, as we know from his notorious review "Mr. Whitman" of *Drum Taps* which appeared November 16, 1865, in the *Nation*. A few days before Howells' review of Whitman's poems had appeared in the *Round Table* and shortly after he had met James, he wrote to Edmund Clarence Stedman on December 5, 1866, that Whitman was no poet and that he was tired of the whole affair. We can imagine, therefore, that James and Howells discussed and then dismissed the good grey poet as beneath consideration; both were, however, to change their opinions of Whitman's poetry later in life and James was to become ashamed of his early review.[16]

James and Howells showed, however, differences of opinion about such writers as Balzac, Hardy, Tolstoy, and Dostoievsky. James, for example, approved of Balzac but did not like Hardy. Although James undoubtedly had read Howells' tribute to Tolstoy in *My Literary Passions* (1895) and knew of the inspiration the Russian had been to him, James—shortly after writing to his friend on his seventy-fifth birthday—remarked to Hugh Walpole that both Tolstoy and Dostoievsky were "fluid puddings" because of their lack of composition and economy. On August 2, 1913, James, after re-reading *War and Peace*, wrote Walpole that the novel sickened him because of the ugliness and waste which resulted from the vice of careless craftsmanship. When Howells wrote an article about the published letters of James, posthumously published, he had, however, no comment to make.[17]

As we review the literary relationship of Howells and James, we can conclude that Howells, throughout their divergent but successful literary careers, accepted as his standard of judgment of James the one he had himself recommended to the readers of his own colums: "If we take him at all we must take him on his own ground, for clearly he will not come to ours. We must make concessions to him. . . ."

ALBERT MORDELL
Philadelphia

NOTES

[1] The anthologies in which two articles, "James's *Hawthorne*" and "Henry James, Jr." were reprinted respectively, are *Criticism and Fiction and Other Essays* (1959) and *Representative Selections from Howells* (1950) both edited by C. Kirk (Kirk) and R. Kirk. Aid in compiling the present collection was received from the *Bibliography of William Dean Howells* by William Gibson and George Arms (1948).

[2] This letter, as well as all others by James, is published with the permission of the James estate.

[3] Besides the early reviews of Howells, there were notices and reviews by others: G. P. Lathrop, H. W. Preston, T. S. Perry.

[4] James was also fortunate in having James Russell Lowell, another personal friend, review these two early books. The reviews of Lowell agreed with Howells' comments about style, but there were marked differences in the stress upon sundry aspects of James's novels. The reviews of Lowell were collected for the first time in *The Function of the Poet*, edited by Albert Mordell (1920).

[5] Hearn was an admirer of James, if not one of Howells; for his essays about the latter, see "Sins of Genius," "One of Mr. Howells's Realisms," and "Howells on Critics," in *Essays on American Literature*, edited by Albert Mordell.

[6] Oscar Firkins, *William Dean Howells: A Study* (Cambridge, 1924), pp. 301-302.

[7] The influence of Goldoni has been ably proved by James L. Woodress, Jr., in *Howells in Italy* (1952).

[8] Edited by William M. Gibson, this lecture was published by the New York Public Library in 1958.

[9] Howells did not include in *My Mark Twain* a review published anonymously by him in *The New Tribune* in October, 1881, of Twain's *The Prince and the Pauper*. It is also interesting to note that, although Howells included in his collection his review of *Innocents Abroad*, he stated in the first section of the publication that "I forget just what I said in praise of it, but it does not matter."

[10] Everett Carter, *Howells and the Age of Realism* (Philadelphia, 1954), pp. 249-263.

[11] James, *The Princess Casimassima* (1886).

[12] S. E. Bowman, "Les Héroines d'Henry James dans *The Portrait of a Lady* et d'Yvan Tourguéniev dan *A la Veille*," *Etudes Anglaises* (Juin, 1958), pp. 136-149.

[13] Leon Edel, *Henry James: The Untried Years: 1843-1870* (Philadelphia, 1953), p. 275.

[14] Edwin H. Cady, *The Road to Realism* (Syracuse, 1956), p. 86.
[15] *Ibid.*, pp. 86-87.
[16] A few of the later views which Howells expressed about Whitman may be worth recording—and one may add that these are not ones generally entertained today.

In *My Literary Passions* (1895) Howells said that Whitman's formlessness was his fatal defect—one in which lay artistic madness. Whitman was liberal as the casing air, but he was often as vague and intangible; he had a wide heart but he had no bounds, no shape. Howells conceded, however, that he had great moments, noble thoughts, and generous aspirations.

Howells favorably reviewed *November Boughs* in *Harper's Monthly*, February, 1889. He admitted that Whitman had made poetry more natural, but hoped a future editor would remove some few offensive lines. He stated that Whitman had met with the usual unwarranted objections reformers meet—and forgot that he himself had earlier raised objections to his verse—both as to form and content. As Cady has stated in *The Road to Realism* (p. 87), Whitman was gratified by Howells' review of *November Boughs*; and Burroughs called Howells the heir of Whitman and Emerson. Cady states that this pronouncement calls our attention to the development which Howells had made intellectually from 1860 to 1890.

In *Literary Friends and Acquaintances* (1902) Howells remarked that he had pleasant recollections of having met Whitman at Pfaff's in August of 1860 and that he had been impressed by the poet's spiritual purity, his sweet and true soul, and his gentility and benignity. But his verse was not poetry, but the means of poetry: not as valuable in effect as in intention. Whitman was an "imperial anarch." Howells stated that he would not misprize his verse, for he had had moments of pleasure reading it, and that Walt at least made one a partner in his enterprise.

[17] Howells was subject to change of opinions. He came to disapprove even of some of his *Harper's Monthly* articles of the late eighties, and of his *Criticism and Fiction* in part, which included some of them and which he revised in 1910.

In reference to the opinion of James about Tolstoy, as given in the text above, it would be hard to say what Howells thought. Howells was converted to Tolstoy's philosophy as imitating Jesus and practicing literally all his ethical views by reading Tolstoy's *What is to be Love* in the late eighties. Howells did not follow either of them in the maxim "Give all thou hast to the poor". He left an estate of $150,000. He really mistakenly put Tolstoy's philosophy above his art. Incidentally Howells, as far as I am aware, does not mention Nietzsche. On the whole I think we may assume that Howells' views on Tolstoy fluctuated for he did not accept every opinion delivered by him. He performed several *volte-faces* with respect to Tolstoy.

At the risk of a charge of egotism, I quote from James L. Woodress's *Howells and Italy*, p. 111, another instance of *volte-face*.

> "Although Howells began his post-Italian years condemning the deification of Dante, he ended his career attacking those who underestimate the poet. Reviewing Albert Mordell's *Dante and Other Waning Classics* he had only scorn for the theory that such masterpieces as the *Divina Commedia* and *Paradise Lost* were being less and less read because

> medieval scholasticism and seventeenth-century Puritanism were no longer, live issues. In this essay (*Harper's Monthly*, XXXII, May 1916, 960) Howells stated his final position on Dante, a criticism which had shifted between middle age and old age from the historical to the aesthetic."

I wrote a reply to this article entitled, "William Dean Howells and the Classics" and sent it to him. Although he disapproved of the article he suggested publishing it in a magazine like *The Bookman*. This periodical rejected it and it finally appeared in *Stratford Monthly*, pps. 199-205, September 1924, edited by Isaac Goldberg and Henry Schnitkind.

INTRODUCTION

The last two decades witnessed a revival of Henry James's fiction which established him as the aesthetic novelist of the writer and the intellectual; as the foremost American novelist; and as a critic whose prefaces to the New York Edition exerted a tremendous influence upon the criticism and the techniques of the novel. In our decade we are in the midst of a resurgence of interest in and of analytical re-interpretations of the fiction of William Dean Howells, who was one of the first critics to recognize the genius of James, his possible influence upon novelists, and his fight both for realism and for the right of the artist to select what he pleased and to portray it as he chose.

The resurrection from obscurity, if not from ignominy, of the reputation of Howells as a novelist and a critic first began perhaps with the centenary publication of Newton Arvin's "The Usableness of Howells," with Henry Steele Commager's *Selected Writings of William Dean Howells* (1950), and with Clara M. and Rudolf Kirk's *William Dean Howells: Representative Selections* (1950). Since these publications, the following contributions have appeared: Edwin Cady's *The Road to Realism: The Early Years, 1837-1885* (1956) and *The Realist at War: The Mature Years, 1885-1920* (1959); Everett Carter's *Howells and the Age of Realism* (1954); George N. Bennett's *William Dean Howells: The Development of a Novelist* (1959); James Woodress' *Howells and Italy* (1952); Olov W. Fryckstedt's *In Quest of America: A Study of Howells' Early Development as a Novelist* (1958); and Van Wyck

Brooks' *Howells: His Life and Work* (1959). In 1959, the Kirks, indefatigable, scholarly supporters of Howells, also published *Howells Criticism and Fiction and Other Essays.*

In *Discovery of a Genius,* Albert Mordell has collected the hitherto—with a few exceptions—unreprinted articles and reviews which Howells published from 1875 to 1903 about James' fiction. Also assembled, from the published letters of the two authors, are what may be considered the most important comments the two men had made to each other—or in some instances to mutual friends—about their friendship and their fiction. These excerpts have been presented in the preface and in the introductions to the three sections of this volume: the reviews of 1875 to 1881, of 1881 to 1890, and of 1890 to 1903. Although it is regretted that not all the unpublished letters exchanged by James and Howells could be included, those published in this volume indicate the warmth of the friendship which existed for so many decades; their unpublished reactions to each other's works; and their differences of opinion.

Discovery of a Genius fulfills, therefore, the need expressed by Edwin Cady in his essay-review in *The New England Quarterly* of September, 1959, for a publication which would include these writings of Howells which express and exemplify all his "really important insights into James." Mordell's collection also indicates that Howells considered James to be his master although Howard Mumford Jones asserts in "The Disciple Proves Independent: Howells and Lowell" (PMLA, September, 1959) that Howells acknowledged only one man among all "his literary friends and acquaintances" as being his superior—James Russell Lowell. Indeed, the most impressive characteristics of Howells' letters to and his articles about James are the sympathy, the respect, the adulation, and the catholicity of judgment which he humbly offered the writer who, he was certain, would one day share a place in American literature with Hawthorne.

Although we recognize today that Henry James was the most famous writer sponsored by Howells, we have not devoted enough attention to Howells' role in the history of American *belles-lettres* as a critic and editor. As Everett Carter has suggested, so much has for so long been made of Howells' phrase of 1886 about "the smiling aspects" of fiction that we have forgotten that he early recognized, published, and defended the early American realists such as Sarah Orne Jewett, Murfee, De Forest, Weir Mitchell, and Mark Twain and that he aided the naturalists Crane and Norris to publish, respectively, *Maggie* and *McTeague*. Because of the charge that Howells was squeamish, we have also forgotten that he defended such "shocking" foreign publications as Ibsen's *Ghosts*, Zola's *La Terre*, Flaubert's *Madame Bovary*, Tolstoy's *Anna Karenina*, Moore's *Esther Waters*, and Hardy's *Tess of the D'Urbervilles* and *Jude the Obscure*. We have also been prone to minimize the importance of the staunch battle Howells waged against the "babes of romance," despite heated attacks both at home and abroad after his important 1882 article about James's fiction; for in articles after this date Howells the critic sanctioned the development not only of literature "truly nationalist in spirit" but of the psychological, mythological, naturalistic, and humanitarian realists who paved the way for the Sinclair Lewises, Farrells, Steinbecks, and Faulkners of contemporary literature.

Although the naturalists—and also James—condemned Howells for his limited presentation of life, we must remember —as Dreiser did not—that the mores of his early environment, his own experiences, his editorial responsibilities, and his desire not to alienate women readers (who formed a vociferous, often censorious majority) influenced his portrayal. More importantly, however, we must recall that Howells, who first exalted American life, became—after his experiences with Tolstoy's fiction, his courageous defense of the condemned Chicago Haymarket Rioters, his reading of Edward Bellamy's *Looking Backward*, and his support of the Bellamy movement—as astute a social critic in his fiction as Dreiser, John Hay, or Henry Adams were in theirs and a novelist who, in *The Landlord at Lion's Head, The Shadow of a Dream*, and *The Son of Royal Langbrith*, certainly did not ignore sex. A thorough study of the symbolism of the novels of Howells may well show that he was not so shallow nor so narrow as many novelists and critics of his day and of ours have deemed him. Such a discovery would, however, not be so shocking to those who have studied his critical comments about the relationship of truth, beauty, and ethics.

Although Howells became a critic with some reluctance (for he would have preferred to have devoted himself wholly to writing fiction), he was determined to "break the images of false gods and mishapen heroes, to take away the poor silly toys that many grown people would like to play with," (15) and to support—instead of romanticism—"the truthful treatment of material" both in his columns and in his fiction. His desire for a veritable presentation of life was without doubt due to his development from a travel writer to a novelist; his association with James Russell Lowell, whom he considered one of the earliest, finest realists, and with Henry James; and his reading of Italian, Spanish, Russian, and French writers.

As a realist who was also a critic, Howells established his critical standards and his own definitions of terms. In *Criticism and Fiction* (1891),[1] which he too hastily assembled from published articles, Howells included his essay about the task

[1] Unless otherwise indicated, the quotations in this introduction are from Clara M. and Rudolf Kirk, eds., *Howells Criticism and Fiction and Other Essays* (New York, 1959). The numbers inserted in the text are references to the pages of this volume.

of the critic which he had written as a result of reading Frederic William Farrar's "Literary Criticism," an article which had appeared in 1890 in the *Forum* and which Howells had found "very much to his liking"—"much like his own" opinions. In his article, Howells carefully delineated what the critic should not and should do.

In passages which many of today's critics would profit from reading and then practicing, Howells warned that critics too frequently felt that their task was "to wield the tomahawk." (20) He also asserted that "in no other relation of life is so much brutality permitted by civilized society as in the criticisms of literature and the arts." Critics, wrote Howells as he conveniently cited Farrar's charges, too frequently judged writers without considering their aims; condemned a writer because of personal prejudice or that of their publication; quoted "a phrase or passage apart from the context" and thereby misrepresented the book or magnified "careless expressions into important faults." (28) In words reminiscent of those written recently by Robert Graves in *Five Pens in Hand,* Howells charged that too often the critic hoped to "show his wit, if not his learning, to strive to eclipse the author under review rather than illustrate him. He has not yet caught on to the fact that it is really no part of his business to display himself. . . ." (21)

In this and other articles of *Criticism and Fiction* and in his review of 1878 of James's *French Poets and Novelists,* Howells asserted that the critic had to be analytical, systematic, and dispassionate and that his criticism should not be mere suggestive *causerie* based upon prejudices or "contradictory impressions." His criticism should display that he had scientifically identified the "species" or class and then explained "how and where the specimen is imperfect and irregular." (2) The critic's task, therefore, was one of "observing, recording, and comparing"; of "analyzing the material . . . and then synthesizing the impressions" (27)—and of expressing them with "modesty and candor and impartiality." (25)

Howells stated also that the scientific—Darwinian—critics should not judge a book by comparing it with past literary models, for such comparison would be conducive to their establishing principles which would cause literature to "travel in a vicious circle" and make the critics incapable of "conceiving the original except as the abnormal." Such comparative criticism led the critics to condemn what was "fresh and vital in literature" and to fight the "new good thing in behalf of the good old thing." As a result of using standards of the past, the critics "invariably fostered and encouraged the tame, the trite, the negative"; and such writers as Keats, Wordsworth, and Browning had received delayed recognition because their works had contained unexpected, unwonted qualities "to which the crtical perceptions and habitudes had painfully to adjust themselves." (27-29)

To Howells the ideal, scientific critic did not try to "direct literature" on the basis of past performances or to establish literary principles; for he was a student of the laws of the mind and of "its generic history" who realized that literature was "a plant which springs from the nature of a people, and draws its forces from their life, and that its root is in their character, and that it takes form from their will and taste." (31) He considered the author "as not in any wise on trial before him, but as a reflection of this or that aspect of life" (23) which "it is his privilege, his high duty to interpret;" (12) for "literature and art . . . the expression of life . . . are to be judged by . . . their fidelity to it." (11) The scientific critic searched the book, therefore, for its truth to life—truth to the "motives, the impulses, the principles that shape the life of actual men and women." (49)

Howells himself did not limit the scope of the realistic writer, for he declared in almost transcendental, mystical terms that the realist found nothing in life that was insignificant for "all tells for destiny and character; nothing that God has made is contemptible. He can not look upon human life and declare this thing or that thing unworthy of notice, any more than the scientist can declare a fact of the material world beneath the dignity of his inquiry. He feels in every nerve the equality of things and the unity of men; his soul is exalted, not by vain shows and shadows and ideals, but by realities, in which alone the truth lives." (15)

Howells demanded, therefore, that realistic "fiction cease to lie about life"; that it "portray men and women as they are, actuated by the motives and the passions in the measure we all know"; that it "leave off painting dolls and working them by means of springs and wires"; that it show "the different interests in their true proportions"; that "it forbear to preach pride and revenge, folly and insanity, egotism and prejudice, but frankly own these for what they are, in whatever figures and occasions they appear"; that it "not put on fine literary airs" but that it "speak the dialect, the language, that most Americans know—the language of unaffected people everywhere. . . ." (51) If realistic fiction attained these objectives, it would not be "the cold grave of the Beautiful" that "effete romanticism" had become but accomplish what romanticism had once sought to accomplish when it had battled against "effete classicism": "to widen the bounds of sympathy, to level every barrier against aesthetic freedom, to escape from the paralysis of tradition. . . . to assert that fidelity to experience and probability of motive are essential conditions of a great imaginative literature." (14-5)

To understand and appreciate fully the catholicity of Howells as a realist and a critic, we must consider the relationship—as he saw it—of truth, beauty, ethics, and aesthetics. As one who heartily adopted Keats's statement that "Beauty is truth, truth beauty," (11) Howells stated that, if "authorized to address any word directly to novelists," he would advise that they should not be troubled by standards or ideals" but try to be "faithful and natural"—and to "remember that there is no greatness, no beauty, which does not come from truth to you own knowledge of things. . . ." (69) In his discussion of Emerson's plea for the study of the common (40, 41) and of Edmund Burke's essay on the sublime and the beautiful—which he considered "a very modern work"—Howells stated that both these men had pointed out that "an easy observation of the most common, sometimes of the meanest things, in nature will give the truest lights, where the greatest sagacity and industry that slights such observation must leave us in the dark, or, what is worse, amuse and mislead us by false lights." (11)

Howells did not, therefore, deny the existence of ugliness nor of "vicious love beneath the surface of our society"; (71) in fact, he stated that "the ugly delights as well as the beautiful." (10) He wrote: "Possibly there is no absolute ugly, no absolutely beautiful; or possibly the ugly contains always an element of the beautiful better adapted to the general appreciation than the more perfectly beautiful." (10) He did not, however, wholly approve of Norris' *McTeague* as a "true picture of life" because it omitted beauty; (277) and in other instances he condemned the portrayal of the ugly or the nasty for the achievement of "cheap effects" or for mercenary reasons. (71)

Just as Howells established the relationship between beauty and truth, so did he depict that among truth, ethics, and aesthetics. In his discussion of the preface to *Pepita Ximenez* in which Valera, the author, advocated "art for art's sake" and condemned novels which proved theses, Howells asserted that, if it were true that the " 'object of a novel should be to charm through a faithful representation of human actions and human passions, and to create by this fidelity to nature a beautiful work' " and if " 'the creation of the beautiful' " was solely the purpose of art, the effect would be more than this. He argued that, until men were resolved "into abstract qualities," "the finest effect of the 'beautiful' will be ethical 'and not aesthetic merely. Morality penetrates all things, it is the soul of all things. Beauty may clothe it . . . whether it is false morality and evil soul, or whether it is true and a good soul. In the one case the beauty will corrupt, and in the other it will edify, and in either case it will infallibly and inevitably have an ethical effect, now light, now grave, according as the thing is light or grave. We cannot escape from this; we are shut up to it by the very conditions of our being." (42)

No one, wrote Howells as he cited and discussed the preface of *Sister Saint Sulpice* by Valdes, could read a " 'naturalistic book without . . . a vivid desire to escape' from the wretched world depicted in it, 'and a purpose, more or less vague, of helping to better the lot and morally elevate the abject beings who figure in it.' " For this reason, naturalistic fiction was not " 'immoral in itself, for then it would not merit the name of greatness, no beauty, which does not come from truth to your art; for though it is not the business of art to preach morality, still I think that, resting on a divine and spiritual principle, like the idea of the beautiful, it is perforce moral.' " (33)

Although Howells believed that the novelist should be—like Turgenev and James—objective in his presentation and that he should not—like Thackeray and Trollope—preach to the reader, he asserted that the writer should "paint such facts of character and custom as he finds so strongly that their relative value in his picture will be at once apparent to the reader without a word of comment." (228) He also stated that what the writer should and could do "ethically, is to make us take thought of ourselves, and look to it whether we have in us the making of this or that wrong, whether we are hypocrites, tyrants, pretenders, shams . . .; whether our most unselfish motives are not really secret shapes of egotism; whether our convictions are not mere brute acceptations; whether we believe what we profess; whether when we force good to a logical end we are not doing evil." (161)

If the novelist accomplished this objective, he—like Tolstoy—converged the ethical and aesthetical principles and transmuted "the atmosphere of a realm hitherto supposed unmoral into the very air of heaven", and his fiction did not contain "those base and cruel lies which cheat us into belief that wrong may sometimes be right through passion, or genius, or heroism." (172-3) If a book contained "truth, which necessarily includes the highest morality and the highest artistry—this truth given, the book cannot be wicked and cannot be weak. . . ." (40) Furthermore, wrote Howells, as he discussed Tolstoy's story of marriage for lust, *Kreutzer Sonata,* "there was not a moment of indecency or horror" in it which was not "purifying and wholesome." After citing Tolstoy's statement that in Maupassant's fiction "the truth can never be immoral," Howells stated that in Tolstoy's fiction it could "never be anything but moral." (173)

If a novel lacked truth, Howells asserted that "all graces of style and feats of invention and cunning construction" would be so "many superfluities of naughtiness." He was not opposed to artistic presentation, but he felt that without truth such a quality was "the bedizenment of the wanton" and that with truth artistry came "naturally" and graced it "without solicitation." He stated that in the "whole range of fiction, we know of no true picture of life—that is, of human nature—which is not also a masterpiece of literature, full of divine and natural beauty." (49) Howells mentioned frequently, for example, the *Personal Memoirs* of U. S. Grant as being simply and straightforwardly written, as being "couched in the most unpretentious phrase, with never a touch of grandiosity or attitudinizing, familiar, homely in style," and yet as forming a "great piece of literature, because great literature is nothing more nor less than the clear expression of minds that have something great in them, whether religion, or beauty, or deep experience." (45) To Howells, aesthetic problems had not the significance which they had to James!

Because of his desire for truthful portrayals, Howells also made distinctions between immoral and unmoral fiction. To him immoral fiction was that "which, under a glamour of something spiritual and beautiful and sublime," portrayed "vices in which we are allied to the beasts." Romantic novels which "tickle our prejudices and lull our judgment, or that coddle our sensibilities or pamper our gross appetites for the marvelous" were neither immoral nor unmoral; but they were "innutritious," they clogged "the soul with unwholesome vapors of all kinds," and they weakened "the moral fibre." They also made their readers indifferent to " 'plodding perseverance and plain industry' and to 'matter-of-fact poverty and commonplace distress.' " Among such novels Howells classified those which depicted love as the most important interest in life—or those which stressed that all things must be sacrified to duty. (47)

Howells, in discussing Goethe, defined the unmoral novel as a "kind of metaphysical lie against righteousness and commonsense" which could mislead the reader. (42) His test of unmoral fiction was: "If a novel flatters the passions, and exalts them above the principles, it is poisonous; it may not kill, but it will certainly injure; and this test alone will exclude an entire class of fiction, of which eminent examples will occur to all. Then the whole spawn of so-called unmoral romances, which imagine a world where the sins of the sense are unvisited by the penalties following swift or slow, but inexorably sure, in the real world, are deadly poison: these do kill." (47) Howells did not, as his comments about the endings of James' novels indicate, believe that the novelist had, however, to punish his evil characters and reward his good ones in the fashion of Goldsmith.

As we review Howells' statements about realism of the commonplace, we find, therefore, that he did not limit the novelist to consideration of the "smiling aspects of life" but that he asked that he be the slave neither of "decency" nor of "indecency;" he only asked that truth be depicted in proportion to its existence. Because of the understanding of Howells' view of the relationship of truth, beauty, and ethics, we can also comprehend why he could accept the naturalism of Zola but not his romanticism and why he could write in 1895 in his review of George Moore's *Celibates* that, although the novel should not be read by young girls, the quality which gave the stories such importance was "their naked truth, which is very, very naked now and then. Sometimes the nakedness abashes, sometimes it appalls. . . ." For the same reason he could also state that, although one might not be able to "praise at every point" and although one might convict it of errors of taste, or even of propriety," *Esther Waters* was a work of art which made one have a "distinct hope" for English fiction and "a great hope" for Moore.

Howells defended the naturalists—but he also defended the novelist who, like himself, might be attacked as prudish when certain "experiences happened not to come" within the scheme of his novel or when he felt "it was all the more faithfully representative of the tone of modern life in dealing with love that was chaste, and with passion so honest that it could be openly spoken of before the tenderest society bud at dinner." Howells also stated that the novelist "might say that the guilty intrigue, the betrayal, the extreme flirtation even, was the exceptional thing in life, and unless the scheme of the story necessarily involved it, that it would be bad art to lug it in, and as bad taste to introduce such topics in a mixed company." (70)

As his articles and reviews of James indicate, as well as the material included in *Criticism and Fiction* and other essays, Howells felt that, if novels were written only for the perusal of married women or of men, the subject matter could be unrestrained; he admitted, however, that in America most of the readers were ladies and "very many of them, if not most, of those ladies are young girls." He did not wish to deprive the older, mature people of literature they could safely enjoy; but, like today's psychiatrist Dr. Fredric Wertham, he pondered the effect books might have which were not immoral but "not wholly decent, as certain well-known facts of life are not." He concluded that such a book as Moore's *Celibates* "could not do them [young girls] any harm, but its bold knowledge might leave a stain in the mind. . . ."

Although we have sufficiently defined what Howells meant by realism, truth, beauty, ethics, aesthetics, and immoral or unmoral fiction, we should consider—for easier comprehension of the reviews and articles which he wrote about James's fiction—his definitions of "romance" and "novel;" his concern with aspects of the novel; and, in passing, his use of the terms "romantic," "poetic," "petting," "effectism," "stage play."

Howells derived or borrowed his definitions of romance and novel from the preface to *The House of Seven Gables* in which Hawthorne had defined the novel as being limited to fidelity "not merely to the possible, but to the probable and ordinary course of man's experience." The romance, however, while it had to be observant of the "truth of the human heart," permitted the writer a "certain latitude both as to its fashion and material, which he would not have felt himself entitled to assume had he professed to be writing a novel." He could in the romance present basic truths or realities "under circumstances . . . of the writer's own choosing or creation. If he thinks fit, also, he may so manage his atmospherical medium as to bring out or mellow the lights and deepen and enrich the shadows of the picture."

In his romances Hawthorne imaginatively portrayed human problems; his situations, therefore, were often strange or idealized—but not too exotic—and his style was often poetic in cadence and in diction. To Howells the type of romance written by Hawthorne was "of the finer kind of romance," and he urged James to write in his fashion. When Howells reviewed James's *Hawthorne,* he reprimanded him for confusing the terms "romance" and "novel" in his discussion of Hawthorne's fiction. When James turned from the writing of romances such as "A Romance of Old Clothes" and "A Passionate Pilgrim" to the writing of novels, Howells regretted his decision and the loss of his poetic creation of atmosphere, imagination, and "beautiful invention." To Howells, such writers as Zola, Hardy, Verga, and Björnson were also poetic because they saw beauty in facts and "conceived of reality poetically." (157)

Howells accepted the "fantastic romance" and the "historical romance" as entertaining escapist reading which might incidentally teach something (56); but he battled against the romantic novels which, in his excellent passage about the real versus the ideal grasshopper (13), he declared lacked any relationship to life itself: to the motives that really prompted people, to the complexities of man, and to the incidents most common in the lives of the majority. Like Flaubert in *Madame Bovary,* Howells believed that romantic fiction could be injurious to the reader because it lied about human nature and the society which people should know and understand. (46-7) Howells, who desired the "natural, honest grasshopper" portrayed in fiction, found Milly Theale of James's *Wings of the Dove* too idealized; he did, however, think that James had done a remarkable job in portraying a woman of her type and background.

To Howells plots which were highly contrived, which were filled with incredible or startling events, which violated reality, and which made the characters puppets of circumstances and thereby sacrificed character for incident were romantic—and he called such plots "effectism," "effectist," "faking," "fables," "stories," and "stage plays." Like James, Howells believed that "the true plot comes out of the character; that is the man does not result from the things he does, but the things he does result from the man, and so plot comes out of character; plot aforethought does not characterize" as the romantics thought it did—but some, Howells admitted, were, like Dickens, capable of making it seem so. (99) Today we would prefer the more cogent definition of James, with which Howells would not quibble, that "character is incident and incident is character."

As may be deduced from the expression Howells employed to indicate his disgust with romantic plots and incidents, he denounced the dramas of his day because of their romanticism; but he, like James, sponsored the dramatic presentation of the fiction of Turgenev. In *My Literary Passions,* Howells stated that the Russian's fiction was "to the last degree dramatic. The persons are sparely described and briefly accounted for, and left to transact their affair, whatever it is, with the least possible comment or explanation from the author. The effect flows naturally from their characters, and when they have done or said a thing you conjecture why as unerringly as you would if they were people you knew outside a book. I had already conceived the possibility of this from Björnson. . . ." In his essay "Leo Tolstoy" (1897), Howells wrote that Turgenev "had so perfected the realistic methods that the subtlest analysis of character had become the essence of drama" and that "the effect sought and produced is the most ethical, the process . . . splendidly aesthetical. . . ." (175).

Howells appreciated these same qualities in James's fiction, and he thought that James's essay about Turgenev was one of the finest included in *French Poets and Novelists*. Because he believed that James's objective, dramatic presentation and his clever use of the point of view had contributed to the misunderstanding of his females—such as Daisy Miller—Howells not only explained but praised his methods to the readers who had deemed James un-American. In his reviews and articles, Howells extolled the impartiality of his narration which he contrasted to the "petting," the "caressing epithets," and the moralizing and sentimentalizing of Thackeray, Trollope, and Balzac.

Although Howells made it clear that he often had difficulty solving the problems which James's later fiction presented, he declared that he enjoyed the puzzle and did not resent the fact that the author trusted the intelligence of the reader. Though he had wondered why James had ended *The American* as he had and though he had pondered the reaction of the public to the unfinished stories of James's novels, Howells finally decided that the unfinished ending was life-like and was the one contribution Goethe had made to the science of fiction. (17-8) What Howells did not want was an ending which would be false to life and, therefore, to art. (43)

As we survey the reviews and articles which Howells wrote about James's fiction, we find that he devoted the most space—in the order mentioned—to the patriotic Americanism and to the originality of James's international women who had not been well received by American female readers; to his methods of narration; to the modern qualities of his fiction; to his ethical delicacy, to his changing style; to his forthcoming place in American literature; and to the limited audience to which his fiction would appeal. Although James was not yet known "to the ignorant masses of educated people," he was, wrote Howells in 1901, "one of the greatest masters of fiction who has ever lived." In 1903 he stated: "Here you have the work of a great psychologist, who has the imagination of a poet, the wit of a keen humorist, the conscience of an impeccable moralist, the temperament of a philosopher, and the wisdom of a rarely experienced witness of the world. . . ."

Despite the fact that Howells established the bases of most critical and analytical approaches to James and that he fought a long, valiant battle against "effete romanticism," he summarized his critical career as having been a "losing fight"; for he thought that "the monstrous rag-baby of romanticism" was as "firmly in the saddle as it was before the joust began, and that it always will be, as long as the children of men are childish." Had Howells lived but a few years longer, he would have perceived that he had won the battle of realism; had he lived for two more decades, he would have witnessed the recognition he so desired James to have—recognition which he had so astutely and generously been one of the first in giving and certainly the most constant in bestowing.

SYLVIA E. BOWMAN

Associate Professor of English
Indiana University

PART ONE
Howells' Early Reviews of James
1875-1881

INTRODUCTION

Howells' first review of Henry James's fiction was of *A Passionate Pilgrim and Other Tales,* and it was published anonymously in the *Atlantic* of April, 1875. When Howells wrote this review he was the editor who, when consulted by his "kindly chief" J. T. Fields in 1866 about accepting a story by James, had replied that he desired not only to publish "Poor Richard" but to obtain all the stories he could get from its author. Howells had also by 1875 established himself as a writer, for he had published *Venetian Life* (1866), which James Russell Lowell had complimented highly; *Italian Journeys* (1867); *Suburban Sketches* (1871); *Their Wedding Journey* (1872); *A Chance Acquaintance* (1873); *A Foregone Conclusion* (1875); and, of course, his campaign biography of Lincoln.

When Howells' review of James's collection appeared, *Roderick Hudson* was running serially in the *Atlantic* which had already published three other of James's pieces. James had also, however, published his first story in the *Continental Monthly,* one in *Galaxy,* and his "Nassau W. Senior's *Essay in Fiction*" in the October, 1864, issue of the *North American Review* which also included Howells' "Recent Italian Comedy." Articles later collected by Howells in *Italian Journeys* and reviews written by James had also appeared simultaneously in *The Nation;*[1] and James had written anonymous reviews of two books by Howells—*The Italian Journeys*[2] and *A Foregone Conclusion*[3]—and a signed review of his poems.[4]

To the readers of the reviews the two men wrote about each other's works, there could be no knowledge—as there could be among those of the inner literary circle—of the fact that the two men had been since 1866 close friends who walked and talked together, who exchanged letters, and who commented about each other in letters to their other friends. After James's death, Howells wrote to Percy Lubbock that he could "scarcely exaggerate the intensity of" his "literary association" with James. It had "included," he wrote, "not only what he [James] was doing and thinking himself in fiction, and criticism of whatever he was reading, but what other people were trying to do in American magazines."[5]

When or how the two writers first met is not certain. James himself left no record of the momentous occasion in *Notes of a Son and Brother*, but he recorded his recollection of the joy he had experienced when Howells had accepted his story "Poor Richard" which appeared in the summer of 1867 in the *Atlantic.* Howells also remarked in a letter to Stedman in December, 1866, that he had this story which aroused his interest in James; and, because of this comment, F. W. Dupee has surmised that this story resulted in the acquaintance of the two men. Since James recalled that he and Howells knew each other in the summer of 1866 and since the story must have arrived in Howells' office in the latter part of the year, it seems logical to conclude that there must have been some other way the men met—perhaps in the home of mutual friends.

No matter how the writers met, they saw each other from 1866 until February, 1869, when James sailed for Europe. They also visited with each other when James returned to the United States in April, 1870, to remain there until May, 1872. In the autumn of 1874 he once more returned to his own country where he spent part of his time in New York before returning to Europe in the autumn of 1875. During the period from 1869 to the fall of 1875, James spent almost three years in the United States; and he often visited with Howells with whom he had corresponded while abroad. Since all their letters have not been published, there are, therefore, few easily available records of the events of these European-American years of James as they relate to his friendship with Howells.

The first letter which records their intimacy was written by Howells to Edmund Stedman on December 5, 1866. In this epistle, Howells remarked that he and James had had one of their famous walks the evening before and that, during its "two or three hours," they had "settled the true principles of literary art." He then remarked that James was a "very earnest fellow," "extremely gifted," and "gifted enough to do better than any one has yet done toward making us a real American novel."

On August 10, 1867, Howells wrote an interesting comment to Charles Eliot Norton about his frequent visits with James and his fear that his friend would have difficulty creating an audience for his type of fiction. Howells stated that James had written another story for his publication and that he thought it admirable—but he also admitted that he did "not feel sure of the public any longer" since the *Nation* had not seen "the merit of '*Poor Richard*'." Whatever James's troubles might be in creating his reading public, Howells felt, however, that he had every element of success in fiction and that he had written scenes of remarkable strength in "Poor Richard."

Howells' enjoyment of James's company was also expressed on November 23, 1868, to Charles Eliot Norton when he described walking with James to the Botanical Gardens and sitting in the sun on the "edge of a hotbed of violets" as "the last favor of fortune." There was nothing better than punching "one's cane into a sandy path," wrote Howells, if one had, of course, "good company."

The first letter we can record of Howells to James is of

June 26, 1869, in which he apologized for his silence and stated that the resentment engendered by James' delay in writing to him had been "melted away by the air of homesickness" in his letter and that he had really flattered himself that "there was some reason why" James "should be so fond of" him. In his comments about James's literary works, Howells stated that the "Light Man"[6] had fascinated him and that he was one of James's "best worst ones." He wished that he had published it in the *Atlantic* although he felt that it was "good policy" for James to send something now and then to *Galaxy*.

Howells also commented in this letter about the reaction to *Gabrielle de Bergerac*[7] which was "thought well of by those whose good opinions ought not to be of any consequence but is" and which promised to make "a greater impression than anything else" James had done for the *Atlantic*. The story was "universally praised;" Mrs. Howells, "a difficult critic," had declared the story to be "really magnificent"; and there seemed at last "to be a general waking-up" to James's merits. Howells then added that when James's fame was as great as Hawthorne's, he was not to forget "who was the first, warmest and truest of your admirers."[8] Howells was not content to report the reactions to *Gabrielle* to James, for he wrote on August 24, 1869, to J. T. Fields, the editor of the *Atlantic*, that this work was to the general reading public a "great gain upon all that" James had done before.

When Henry James returned from Europe, Howells wrote on May 22, 1870, to James Russell Lowell that his return and a call that John R. Dennett (the critic who had written adversely about "Poor Richard") had made upon him "were the greatest events of life for him"—unless the fact that his son had learned "a new word every day" was greater.

During the 1870's James wrote on May 20, 1870, to Grace Norton a letter (published in Edel's *Select Letters of Henry James*) in which he commented that he was attending Howells' lectures about Italian literature which were being given at Boylston Hall and that he sat with his eyes closed listening to the sweet Italian names. In April, 1871, James wrote to Elizabeth Boot, the wife of Frank Duveneck and the model for Pansie in *The Portrait of a Lady,* that he was to meet Bret Harte at the Howells home. He also thanked her for her compliment about "A Passionate Pilgrim" which had appeared in the March-April, 1871, issues of the *Atlantic.*

On November 27, 1870, James wrote to Grace Norton rather derogatory comments about Howells after the publication of *Their Wedding Journey.* James called his friend "poor Howells" and "a melancholy spectacle" in that "his charming style and refined intentions are so poorly and meagrely served by our American atmosphere. There is no more inspiration in an American journey than *that*! Thro' thick and thin I continue however to enjoy him—or rather thro' thin and thinner. There is a little divine spark of fancy which never quite gives out." James then expressed the opinion that Howells possessed a second or third rate talent which would make him always a "small but genuine writer" but that he was "destined to fade slowly and softly away in self-repetition and reconcilement to the commonplace."[9]

After Howells' *Suburban Sketches* appeared, James wrote on January 16, 1871 to Charles Eliot Norton:

> "In Cambridge I see Arthur Sedgwick [Mrs. Charles Eliot Norton's brother] and Howells. . . . Howells edits, and observes and produces—the latter in his own particular line with more and more perfection. His recent sketches in the *Atlantic* collected into a volume, belong, I think, by the wondrous cunning of their manner, to be very good literature. He seems to have resolved himself, however, [into] one who can write solely of what his fleshly eyes have seen; and for this reason I wish he were located where they would rest upon richer and fairer things than

> his immediate landscape. Looking about for myself, I conclude that the face of nature and civilization in this our country is to a certain point a very sufficient literary field. But it will yield its secrets only to a really grasping imagination. This I think Howells lacks. (Of course *I* don't.) To write well and worthily of American things one need even more than elsewhere be a master. But unfortunately, one is less. . . ."[10]

In other letters which he wrote to his brother and to his friends, James also made more candid critical assessments of Howells than he ever made directly to him or in his reviews of his publications. On August 9, 1871, James wrote to Charles Eliot Norton that Howells, "now monarch absolute" of the *Atlantic,* had a talent that improved in quality but not in application. He had, thought James, little intellectual curiosity; he did not care to read Sainte-Beuve; and as to his admirable style—with that he did not know what to do! Interestingly enough, James remarked in this letter that other younger, American writers seemed lacking in their desire to do their best —but that he himself found that his love of art kept pace with his growth.[11]

In contrast to the remarks which James made about his friend is the respectful, nostalgic letter which Howells wrote to James on September 1, 1872. After expressing his certainty that James's "Guest's Confession" would win favor and his intention of publishing the "Florentine Story,"[12] Howells expressed his regret that James had not prepared a volume of short stories for publication for he felt that he could "make a successful book of the romantic tales"[13] and that he could have assembled "the liking and respect" he had won with such a collection. Howells also remarked that the *Nation* had brought him regularly James's letters;[14] that he had liked them, as he liked "everything" of James; but that he thought he "tended a little too much to the metaphysical expression of travel, as opposed to the graphic." Howells admitted, however, that when he had objected to this characteristic before, he had heard Lowell praise it.

In the postscript of this letter Howells reported that the weather was "so fresh" that he had lighted a fire in the stove that morning and that, if James were only there, they could have the "longest, briskest walk of the year, without discomfort." He then reflected upon the passage of the years which had left so little behind them; and, as he recalled the walks they had taken, he remarked that he and James seemed "less substantial in the past than the shadows of the clouds that drifted over the same autumnal paths." He then wrote that "sometimes the whole intolerable mystery of the thing comes over me suffocatingly—" and that he did not "feel as if a first-class notice in the *Nation* were worth striving for." After adding that this was, of course, "a disease," he wished James happiness and hoped that he was "putting by a store of the honey" he was finding on "those Swiss mountain sides."

On March 10, 1873, Howells wrote James about the success of "The Madonna of the Future," which, according to a letter to Henry from his father, Howells had censored because he had felt "one episode . . . as being risky for the magazine." Although Henry James, Sr., felt that "Howells *in general* is too timid," he admitted that he, his wife, and his daughter had agreed that the censored section was rather "scary" or "musky."[16] Howells commented that he had been impatient to tell James not only how much he had liked "The Madonna" but about "the undissenting voice of acclaim" with which it "had been hailed"—even though the "Delphic Dennett"[17] had remained silent. To Howells the success was justified because of the solidity and excellence of the work; and he reported that all liked the "well-managed pathos of it, the dissertations on pictures, the tragic, most poetical central fact, and I hope that many feel with me its unity and completeness." To him "every figure in it" was a real character" who had some "business there." He admitted, however, that he felt that the sole blemish was James's "insistence on the cats and monkey philosophy" which he should not have permitted to appear as a refrain at the close; his doing so had "marred the fine harmony of what went before. Howells then remarked that he had James's "Roman Romance"—"The Last of the Valerii"—and that he liked it and intended to print it very soon (he did not however publish it until January, 1874).

When Howells' *A Chance Acquaintance* was being serialized in the *Atlantic* from January to June in 1873, James wrote Howells a letter of praise which has not been published—nor has the reply which Howells wrote to him on May 12, 1873. On June 22, 1873, James wrote a reply to Howells' May letter in which he thanked him "for everything; for liking my writing and for being glad I like yours." The following excerpt doubtless refers to the reference Howells had made in his letter to the orchards by Fresh Pond, for James wrote:

> "Your letter made me homesick: and when you told of the orchards by Fresh Pond I hung my head for melancholy. . . . From my window I look out across the rushing Aar. . . . But I would rather be taking up my hat and stick and going to invite myself to tea with you. . . . I heard from my mother a day or two that your book [*A Chance Acquaintance*] is having a sale—bless it! I haven't yet seen the last part and should like to get the volume as a whole. . . . Your fifth part I extremely relished; it was admirably touched. I wish the talk in which the offer was made had been given (instead of the mere résumé,) but I suppose you had good and sufficient reasons for doing as you did. But your work is a success and Kitty a creation I have envied you greatly, as I read, the delight of feeling her grown so real and complete, so true and charming. I think, in bringing her through with such unerring felicity, your imagination has *fait ses preuves*."[18]

On December 5, 1873, Howells wrote James a letter of particular interest because it indicates the relationship of the two critics. Howells had met James's mother on the street and she had told him that her son had written a review of Howells' poetry for the *North American Review,* that James had been anticipated by another " 'party' ", that she had the review, and that Howells might read it "before it was sent off to seek its fortune." Howells stated that he had read it with "great consolation and thankfulness, for the leaf that has been commonly bestowed upon my poetical works by the critics of this continent has not been the laurel leaf—rather rue, or cypress." Howells then promised his friend that he would not forget James's "gracious kindness" and that he hoped he would not be considered immodest to add that James had shown his book of poetry its "first real discernment."

As he had promised to do in his letter of March 10th, Howells then expressed his more considered opinion of "The Last of the Valerii" which he now liked "very much" and thought "excellent" although he admitted that, when he had read it in manuscript, it had not struck him so favorably as it had in print. He also reported that James's "Chain of the Cities" was to be published in the February issue and his "Siena," which Howells thought "charming," was to be in the March number.[19] He then expressed his hope that James would not send any of his stories to *Scribner's,* and he reminded his friend that he had been able to print all the stories James had submitted and would be able to continue to do so. He admitted not only that he had no claim upon James but that *Scribner's* was "trying to lure away all our contributors, with the siren song of Doctor Holland." Howells' "professional pride" was "touched."

During the late 1870's James wrote two important books, *The American* and *Daisy Miller.*[20] Sometime in March, 1877, Howells wrote James a letter which has never been published about *The American*, which he had accepted for serialization in *The Atlantic Monthly*. From the letter of James of March 30, 1877 (published in Edel's *The Selected Letters of Henry James*), it is possible, however to deduce from the defensive remarks the criticisms which Howells had made:

> "I must write you three lines of acknowledgment [but he wrote nearly four printed pages] of your welcome letter. Its most interesting portion was naturally your stricture on the close of my tale, which I accept with saintly meekness. These are matters which one feels about as one may, or as one can, I quite understand that as an editor you should go in for 'cheerful endings'; but I am sorry that as a private reader you are not struck with the inevitability of the *American* dénoument. I fancied that most folks would feel that Mme. de Cintre couldn't, when the finish came marry Mr. N[ewman]!"[21]

When Howells read *Daisy Miller*,[22] he thought more highly of James's ability than ever before. He was also pleased with the publicity the novel received—although much of it was harmful to James—and Howells defended it not only in "The Contributors Club"[23] in February and March, 1879, but also in *Harper's* Bazaar in 1902 with an article which he had already published in *Heroines of Fiction* in 1901. In other reviews, Howells frequently mentioned the misunderstood and castigated *Daisy Miller* when he wrote of James's heroines or of the difficulty of interpreting James because of his objective narration.

When Howells wrote to James Russell Lowell on June 22, 1879, he remarked that James's *Daisy Miller* had "waked up all the women" because they had misconceived its intention and that there had "been a vast discussion in which nobody felt very deeply, and everybody talked very loudly." The discussion had, however, almost divided society into "Daisy Millerites" and "anti-Daisy Millerites"—and he was pleased that this was the situation for he hoped that, by making James "so thoroughly known," the controversy would "call attention in a wide degree to the beautiful work he has been doing so long for very few readers and still fewer lovers." Howells stated that he felt that *Daisy Miller* reflected James's "best touch" and that "his art is an honor to us and his patriotism—which was duly questioned—is of the wholesome kind that doesn't blink our foibles."

In June, 1879, James expressed to Howells his own reactions to the success of *Daisy Miller*:

> "I am delighted to hear of the flourishing condition of my fame in the U.S. and feel as if it were a great shame that I shouldn't be there to reap a little the harvest of my glory. My fame indeed seems to do very well everywhere—the proportions it has acquired here are a constant surprise to me; it is only my fortune that leaves to be desired. . . . I am pledged to write a long novel as soon as possible and am obliged to delay it only because I can't literally afford it. Working slowly and painfully as I do, I need for such a purpose a longish stretch of time during which I am free to do nothing else, and such liberal periods don't present themselves—I have always to keep the pot-a-boiling. The aforesaid fame, expanding through two hemispheres, is represented by a pecuniary equivalent almost grotesquely small. Your account of the vogue of *Daily Miller* and the *International Episode*, for instance, embittered my spirit when I reflected that it had awakened no echo (to speak of) in my pocket."[24]

In 1879 James published *Hawthorne*, a biography which F. O. Matthiessen considered "a landmark in American criticism" and a study more important for the light it sheds upon James's literary objectives than for its penetration of the true significance of Hawthorne's allegories.[25] The book was attacked as unpatriotic because James had commented, as had Hawthorne and Irving before him, that America had no ancient tradition with monuments and cathedrals and therefore could not produce a great literature. When Howells reviewed the biography in February, 1880, he praised it; but he also took James to task for having "over-insisted upon" the fact that Hawthorne was "exquisitely provincial."

When James wrote to Howells about his review, he defended his use of the epithet to which his friend had objected:

> "Your review of my book is very handsome and friendly and commands my liveliest gratitude. Of course your graceful strictures seem to yourself more valid than they do to me. The little book was a tolerably deliberate and meditated performance, and I should be prepared to do battle for most of the convictions expressed. It is quite true I use the word provincial too many times—I hated myself for't, even while I did it (just as I overdo the epithet 'dusky'.) But I don't at all agree with you in thinking that 'if it is not provincial for an Englishman to be English, a Frenchman French, etc., so it is not provincial for an American to be American.' So it is not provincial for a Russian, an Australian, a Portuguese, a Dane, a Laplander, to savour of their respective countries: that would be where the argument would land you. I think it is extremely provincial for a Russian to be a very fine Russian, a Portuguese very Portuguese; for the simple reason that certain national types are essentially and intrinsically provincial. I sympathize even less with your protest against the idea that it takes an old civilization to set a novelist in motion—a proposition that seems to me so true as to be a truism. It is on manners, customs, usages, habits, forms, upon all these things matured and established, that a novelist lives—they are the very stuff his work is made of; and in saying that in the absence of those 'dreary and worn-out paraphernalia' which I enumerate

as being wanting in American society, 'we have simply the whole of human life left,' you beg (to my sense) the question. I should say we had just so much less of it as these same 'paraphernalia' represent, and I think they represent an enormous quantity of it. I shall feel refuted only when we have produced (setting the present high company—yourself and me—for obvious reasons apart) a gentleman who strikes me as a novelist—as belonging to the company of Balzac and Thackeray. Of course, in the absence of this godsend, it is but a harmless amusement that we should reason about it, and maintain that if right were right he should already be here. I will freely admit that such a genius will get on *only* by agreeing with your view of the case—to do something great he must feel as you feel about it. But then I doubt whether such a genius —a man of the faculty of Balzac or Thackeray—*could* agree with you! When he does I will lie flat on my stomach and do him homage—in the very centre of the contributor's club, or on the threshold of the magazine, or in any public place you may appoint!—But I didn't mean to wrangle with you—I meant only to thank you and to express my sense of how happily you turn those things. . . ."[26]

During Howells' editorship of the *Atlantic Monthly* he reviewed or defended five of James's books: *The Passionate Pilgrim and Other Tales, Transatlantic Sketches, French Poets and Novelists, Daisy Miller,* and *Hawthorne*. He probably did not review other of his friend's publications either because he felt that, as editor of the magazine which published them, his comments might be suspect or because he could always *select* someone else to write reviews of or comments about them for "The Contributor's Club."

Although many of the reviews and comments about James's works were anonymous, the signed ones and the *Atlantic Monthly Index* reveal the names of others who reviewed James's books during Howells' editorship. Two of James's novels—*Roderick Hudson* and *The American*—were reviewed by George Parson Lathrop who had assisted Howells in enlivening and in broadening the scope of the *Atlantic.* T. S. Perry, a friend of James, reviewed *Confidence*; Harriet W. Preston, whose translation of Sainte-Beuve's *Portraits of French Women* had been favorably noticed by James, reviewed *Europeans* and *International Episode*; and Horace Scudder wrote about *Washington Square.*

James was also fortunate in having James Russell Lowell, another personal friend, review two of his early books: *The Passionate Pilgrim and Other Tales* and *Transatlantic Sketches.* Lowell's estimate of James agred with Howells', for both critics thought that James had a superb style and was really a poet. Howells, however, stressed the international aspect of James's work; but Lowell wrote that "James deals mainly with problems of character and psychology which spring out of the artifical complexities of society" and that "nowhere does" James "show his fine instinct more to the purpose than in leaving the tragic element of tales to take care of itself, in confining the outward expression of passion within the limits of a decorous amenity."[27]

In approaching the following collection of reviews which Howells wrote about his much-admired friend's works, we must remember that we do so with an advantage not shared by the nineteenth-century reader who had not the opportunity of Stedman or others of the inner literary circle to know about the friendship which existed and meant so much to the two writers. The reader of the periodicals in which the reviews and articles of Howells appeared without doubt considered them to be objective, impartial appraisals written by a stranger—certainly not by an editor who had accepted most of the tales and some of the sketches of his friend for publication.

NOTES

[1] James's first review appeared in the opening number of the *Nation* in the early summer of 1865.

[2] James's review of *Italian Journeys* was in the *North American Review*, January, 1868.

[3] *Ibid.*, January, 1875 (*A Foregone Conclusion*).

[4] *The Nation*, January 6, 1874. These three reviews were collected in *Literary Reviews and Essays of Henry James*, edited by Albert Mordell (1957).

[5] Percy Lubbock, ed., *The Letters of Henry James* (New York, 1920), Vol. I, pp. 10-11.

[6] The "A Light Man" was collected by Albert Mordell in *Master Eustace* (1920).

[7] In spite of the encomiums about *Gabrielle de Bergerac*, James never reprinted it. It was issued in book form in 1918 after being submitted to Boni and Liveright by Albert Mordell, who at that time did not know that Howells had praised it or that Minnie Temple had admired it; their letters had not yet been published.

[8] Needless to say, James never forgot his admirer. He consequently published reviews and articles about him—one of these was the article in *Harper's Weekly*, June 19, 1886.

[9] Edel, *Henry James . . .*, p. 273. Edel documents this letter as of November 27, 1870; but *Their Wedding Journey* was published on December 27, 1871, and had been serialized in the *Atlantic* from July to December, 1871.

[10] Lubbock, ed., *The Letters of Henry James*, Vol. I, pp. 30-31 (ellipses supplied by Mr. Lubbock; perhaps the omitted words were more disparaging). Fifteen years later James, in his general article about Howells published in *Harper's Weekly*, June 19, 1886, and reprinted by Edel and Wilson, wrote glowingly of *Surburban Sketches*. After commenting that Howells had "conferred . . . distinction upon" the *Atlantic*, he remarked that "he wrote the fine series of *Suburban Sketches*, one of the least known of his productions, but one of the most perfect."

James was often prone to change his opinions of books and authors, but usually from favorable to unfavorable as with George Sand, Alphonse Daudet, and Turgenev's *Virgin Soil*. (See *Literary Reviews and Essays by Henry James*, 1957.)

[11] Edel, *Henry James . . .*, p. 276.

[12] The Florentine story was "The Madonna of the Future," reprinted in *A Passionate Pilgrim*. It did not appear in the *Atlantic* in January but in March, 1873.

[13] The first volume of collected tales by James was *A Passionate Pilgrim* (1875). He did not include in it some of the tales which Howells had praised in the excerpts we have quoted. Five tales in it had appeared in the *Atlantic* and one, "Madame de Mauve," in *Galaxy*.

"Guest's Confessions" was printed for the first time in *Travelling Companions* (1919) and "Poor Richard" for the first time in America in *A Landscape Painter* (1920), both volumes collected and edited by Albert Mordell. *Gabrielle de Bergerac* was published for the first time and in a separate volume in 1918. It was suggested to the publisher by Albert Mordell.

[14] The letters to the *Nation* were those reprinted in *Transatlantic Sketches*; a review of it by Howells follows in this collection.

[15] Lowell later anonymously reviewed *Transatlantic Sketches*, as well as *A Passionate Pilgrim*, in the *Nation*. As previously mentioned, these reviews were collected in *The Function of the Poet* (1920).

[16] Henry James, Sr., quoted by F. W. Dupee, *Henry James* (Garden City, 1956), p. 69.

[17] John R. Dennett, who worried Howells because of his comments about "Poor Richard," had also sharply criticized Dr. Oliver Wendell Holmes's novel *The Guardian Angel* which was running serially in the *Atlantic*. Dennett stated that in both authors the physical influence of sex was very perceptible, but that in James's stories it was not only refined but subtle. Holmes wrote, however, like a materialist. (*The Nation*, May 30, 1867. Quoted by Eleanor Tilton, *Amiable Autocrat*, p. 291).

[18] Lubbock, *op. cit.*, Vol. V, pp. 34-35.

[19] Both of these sketches were first collected by James in *Transatlantic Sketches*.

[20] Howells did not review *The American* but G. P. Lathrop did.

[21] In later years in his article about the *Tragic Muse* (1890), Howells conceded that whether or not the characters married was not important.

[22] Perhaps the bibliographical data about *Daisy Miller*, given by Leon Edel and Dan H. Laurence, should be noted. *Daisy Miller* first appeared in periodical form in England in *Cornhill Magazine*, June to July, 1878. It was next copied without authorization in the same summer in *Littell's Living Age* and in the *Home Journal*. It was then published in book form in both paper and cloth covers in November, 1878, by Harper Brothers; later it was published in February, 1879, in England with two other stories by James in two volumes.

[23] Edmond L. Volpe in an article entitled "The Reception of *Daisy Miller*" in *Boston Public Library*, January, 1958 (pp. 58-59), takes it for granted that the two articles in the "Contributor's Club" of the *Atlantic Monthly* of February and March, 1879, which dealt with *Daisy Miller* were by Howells. There is no doubt that this is true, for who else would be so likely to write such a defense as James's friend—and the editor who was publishing him serially? Although bibliographers of Howells may have known that he wrote some of the columns of "The Contributor's Column," they without doubt wanted to be conservative and did not assign them to him. Although Volpe says that these aricles about *Daisy Miller* were attributed to Howells, he does not say by whom; the index of the *Atlantic Monthly* gives the names of anonymous authors but not of those in this column.

[24] Quoted in F. O. Matthiessen's *The James Family* (New York, 1948), p. 501.

[25] *Ibid.*, p. 481.

[26] Lubbock, *op. cit.*, Vol. II, pp. 71-74.

[27] *The Function of the Poet.*

THE PASSIONATE PILGRIM AND OTHER TALES*

Mr. Henry James, Jr., has so long been a writer of magazine stories, that most readers will realize with surprise the fact that he now presents them for the first time in book form. He has already made his public. Since his earliest appearance in The Atlantic people have strongly liked and disliked his writing; but those who know his stories, whether they like them or not, have constantly increased in number, and it has therefore been a winning game with him. He has not had to struggle with indifference, that subtlest enemy of literary reputations. The strongly characteristic qualities of his work, and its instantly recognizable traits, made it at once a question for every one whether it was an offense or a pleasure. To ourselves it has been a very great pleasure, the highest pleasure that a new, decided, and earnest talent can give; and we have no complaint against this collection of stories graver than that it does not offer the author's whole range. We have read them all again and again, and they remain to us a marvel of delightful workmanship. In richness of expression and splendor of literary performance, we may compare him with the greatest, and find none greater than he; as a piece of mere diction, for example, The Romance of Certain Old Clothes in this volume is unsurpassed. No writer has a style more distinctly his own than Mr. James, and few have the abundance and felicity of his vocabulary; the pre-

* *Atlantic Monthly* (April, 1875).

cision with which he fits the word to the thought is exquisite; his phrase is generous and ample. Something of an old-time stateliness distinguishes his style, and in a certain weight of manner he is like the writers of an age when literature was a far politer thing than it is now. In a reverent ideal of work, too, he is to be rated with the first. His aim is high; he respects his material; he is full of his theme; the latter-day sins of flippancy, slovenliness, and insincerity are immeasurably far from him.

In the present volume we have one class of his romances or novelettes: those in which American character is modified or interpreted by the conditions of European life, and the contact with European personages. Not all the stories of this sort that Mr. James has written are included in this book, and one of the stories admitted—The Romance of Certain Old Clothes—belongs rather to another group, to the more strictly romantic tales, of which the author has printed several in these pages; the scene is in America, and in this also it differs from its present neighbors. There is otherwise uncommon unity in the volume, though it has at first glance that desultory air which no collection of short stories can escape. The same purpose of contrast and suggestion runs through A Passionate Pilgrim, Eugene Pickering, The Madonna of the Future, and Madame de Mauves, and they have all the same point of view. The American who has known Europe much can never again see his country with the single eye of his old ante-European days. For good or for evil, the light of the Old World is always on her face; and his fellow-countrymen have their shadows cast by it. This is inevitable; there may be an advantage in it, but if there is none, it is still inevitable. It may make a man think better or worse of America; it may be refinement or it may be anxiety; there may be no compensation in it for the loss of that tranquil indifference to Europe which untraveled Americans feel, or it may be the very mood in which an American may best understand his fellow-Americans. More and more, in any case, it pervades our literature, and it seems to us the mood in which Mr. James's work, more than that of any other American, is done. His attitude is not that of a mere admirer of Europe and contemner of America—our best suffers no disparagement in his stories; you perceive simply that he is most contented when he is able to confront his people with situations impossible here, and you fancy in him a mistrust of such mechanism as the cis-Atlantic world can offer the romancer.

However this may be, his book is well worth the carefullest study any of our critics can give it. The tales are all freshly and vigorously conceived, and each is very striking in a very different way, while undoubtedly A Passionate Pilgrim is the best of all. In this Mr. James has seized upon what seems a very common motive, in a hero with a claim to an English estate, but the character of the hero idealizes the situation: the sordid illusion of the ordinary American heir to English property becomes in him a poetic passion, and we are made to feel an instant tenderness for the gentle visionary who fancies himself to have been misborn in our hurried, eager world, but who owes to his American birth the very rapture he feels in gray England. The character is painted with the finest sense of its charm and its deficiency, and the story that grows out of it is very touching. Our readers will remember how, in the company of the supposed narrator, Clement Searle goes down from London to the lovely old country-place to which he has relinquished all notion of pretending, but which he fondly longs to see; and they will never have forgotten the tragedy of his reception and expulsion by his English cousin. The proprietary Searle stands for that intense English sense of property which the mere dream of the American has unpardonably outraged, and which in his case wreaks itself in an atrocious piece of savagery. He is imagined with an extraordinary sort of vividness which leaves the redness of his complexion like a stain on the memory; and yet we believe we realize better the dullish kindness, the timid sweetness of the not-at-once handsome sister who falls in love with the poor American cousin. The atmosphere of the story, which is at first that of a novel, changes to the finer air of romance during the scenes at Lockley Park, and you gladly accede to all the romantic conditions, for the sake of otherwise unattainable effects. It is good and true that Searle should not be shocked out of his unrequited affection for England by his cousin's brutality, but should die at Oxford, as he does, in ardent loyalty to his ideal; and it is one of the fortunate inspirations of the tale to confront him there with that decayed and reprobate Englishman in whom abides a longing for the New World as hopeless and unfounded as his own passion for the Old. The character of Miss Searle is drawn with peculiar sweetness and firmness; there is a strange charm in the generous devotion masked by her trepidations and proprieties, and the desired poignant touch is given when at the end she comes only in time to stand by Searle's death-bed. Throughout the story there are great breadths of deliciously sympathetic description. At Oxford the author lights his page with all the rich and mellow picturesqueness of the ancient university town, but we do not know that he is happier there than in his sketches of Lockley Park and Hampton Court, or his study of the old London inn. Everywhere he conveys to you the rapture of his own seeing; one reads such a passage as this with the keen transport that the author felt in looking on the scene itself:—

"The little village of Hampton Court stands clustered about the broad entrance of Bushey Park. After we had dined we lounged along into the hazy vista of the great avenue of horse-chestnuts. There is a rare emotion, familiar to every intelligent traveler, in which the mind, with a great, passionate throb, achieves a magical synthesis of its impressions. You feel England; you feel Italy. The reflection for the moment has an extraordinary poignancy. I had known it from time to time in

Italy, and had opened my soul to it as to the spirit of the Lord. Since my arrival in England I had been waiting for it to come. A bottle of excellent Burgundy at dinner had perhaps unlocked to it the gates of sense; it came now with a conquering tread. Just the scene around me was the England of my visions. Over against us, amid the deep-hued bloom of its ordered gardens, the dark red palace, with its formal copings and its vacant windows, seemed to tell of a proud and splendid past; the little village nestling between park and palace, around a patch of turfy common, with its tavern of gentility, its ivy-towered church, its parsonage, retained to my modernized fancy the lurking semblance of a feudal hamlet. It was in this dark, composite light that I had read all English prose; it was this mild, moist air that had blown from the verses of English poets; beneath these broad acres of rain-deepened greenness a thousand honored dead lay buried."

A strain of humor which so pleasantly characterizes the descriptions of the London inn, tinges more sarcastically the admirable portrait of the shabby Rawson at Oxford, and also colors this likeness of a tramp—a fellow-man who has not had his picture better done:—

"As we sat, there came trudging along the road an individual whom from afar I recognized as a member of the genus 'tramp.' I had read of the British tramp, but I had never yet encountered him, and I brought my historic consciousness to bear upon the present specimen. As he approached us he slackened pace and finally halted, touching his cap. He was a man of middle age, clad in a greasy bonnet, with greasy ear-locks depending from its sides. Round his neck was a grimy red scarf, tucked into his waistcoat; his coat and trousers had a remote affinity with those of a reduced hostler. In one hand he had a stick; on his arm he bore a tattered basket, with a handful of withered green stuff in the bottom. His face was pale, haggard, and degraded beyond description,—a singular mixture of brutality and finesse. He had a history. From what height had he fallen, from what depth had he risen? Never was a form of rascally beggarhood more complete. There was a merciless fixedness of outline about him, which filled me with a kind of awe. I felt as if I were in the presence of a personage—an artist in vagrancy.

" 'For God's sake, gentlemen,' he said, in that raucous tone of weather-beaten poverty suggestive of chronic sore-throat exacerbated by perpetual gin,—'for God's sake, gentlemen, have pity on a poor fern-collector!'—turning up his stale dandelions. 'Food hasn't passed my lips, gentlemen, in the last three days.'

"We gaped responsive, in the precious pity of guileless Yankeeism. 'I wonder,' thought I, 'if half a crown would be enough?' And our fasting botanist went limping away through the park with a mystery of satirical gratitude superadded to his general mystery."

Mr. James does not often suffer his sense of the ludicrous to relax the sometimes over-serious industry of his analyses, and when he has once done so, he seems to repent it. Yet we are sure that the poetic value of A Passionate Pilgrim is enhanced by the unwonted interfusion of humor, albeit the humor is apt to be a little too scornful. The tale is in high degree imaginative, and its fascination grows upon you in the reading and the retrospect, exquisitely contenting you with it as a new, fine, and beautiful invention.

In imaginative strength it surpasses the other principal story of the book. In Madame de Mauves the spring of the whole action is the idea of an American girl who will have none but a French nobleman for her husband. It is not a vulgar adoration of rank in her, but a young girl's belief that ancient lineage, circumstances of the highest civilization, and opportunities of the greatest refinement, must result in the noblest type of character. Grant the premises, and the effect of her emergence into the cruel daylight of facts is unquestionably tremendous: M. le Baron de Mauves is frankly unfaithful to his American wife, and, finding her too dismal in her despair, advises her to take a lover. A difficulty with so French a situation is that only a French writer can carry due conviction of it to the reader. M. de Mauves, indeed, justifies himself to the reader's sense of likelihood with great consistency, and he is an extremely suggestive conjecture. Of course, he utterly misconceives his wife's character and that of all her race, and perceives little and understands nothing not of his own tradition:—

"They talked for a while about various things, and M. de Mauves gave a humorous account of his visit to America. His tone was not soothing to Longmore's excited sensibilities. He seemed to consider the country a gigantic joke, and his urbanity only went so far as to admit that it was not a bad one. Longmore was not, by habit, an aggressive apologist for our institutions; but the baron's narrative confirmed his worst impressions of French superficiality. He had understood nothing, he had felt nothing, he had learned nothing; and our hero, glancing askance at his aristocratic profile, declared that if the chief merit of a long pedigree was to leave one so vaingloriously stupid, he thanked his stars that the Longmores had emerged from obscurity in the present century, in the person of an enterprising lumber merchant. M. de Mauves dwelt of course on that prime oddity of ours, the liberty allowed to young girls; and related the history of his researches into the 'opportunities' it presented to French noblemen,—researches in which, during a fortnight's stay, he seemed to have spent many agreeable hours. 'I am bound to admit,' he said, 'that in every case I was disarmed by the extreme candor of the young lady, and that they took care of themselves to better purpose than I have seen some mammas in France take care of them.' Longmore greeted this handsome concession with the grimmest of smiles, and damned his impertinent patronage."

This is all very good character, and here is something from the baron that is delicious:—

"I remember that, not long after our marriage, Madame de Mauves undertook to read me one day a certain Wordsworth,—a poet highly esteemed, it appears, *chez vous.* It seemed to me that she took me by the nape of the neck and forced my head for half an hour over a basin of *soupe aux choux,* and that one ought to ventilate the drawing-room before any one called."

The baron's sister, in her candid promotion of an intrigue between Madame de Mauves and Longmore, we cannot quite account for even by the fact that she hated them both. But Madame de Mauves is the strength of the story, and if Mr. James has not always painted the kind of women that women like to meet in fiction, he has richly atoned in her lovely nature for all default. She is the finally successful expression of an ideal of woman which has always been a homage, perhaps not to all kinds of women, but certainly to the sex. We are thinking of the heroine of Poor Richard, of Miss Guest in Guest's Confession, of Gabrielle de Bergerac in the story of that name, and other gravely sweet girls of this author's imagining. Madame de Mauves is of the same race, and she is the finest,—as truly American as she is womanly; and in a peculiar fragrance of character, in her purity, her courage, her inflexible high-mindedness, wholly of our civilization and almost of our climate, so different are her virtues from the virtues of the women of any other nation.

The Madonna of the Future is almost as perfect a piece of work, in its way, as A Passionate Pilgrim. It is a more romantic conception than Madame de Mauves, and yet more real. Like A Passionate Pilgrim, it distinguishes itself among Mr. James's stories as something that not only arrests the curiosity, stirs the fancy, and interests the artistic sense, but deeply touches the heart. It is more than usually relieved, too, by the author's humorous recognition of the pathetic absurdity of poor Theobald, and there is something unusually good in the patience with which the handsome, common-minded Italian woman of his twenty years' adoration is set before us. Our pity that his life should have slipped away from him in devout study of this vulgar beauty, and that she should grow old and he should die before he has made a line to celebrate her perfection or seize his ideal, is vastly heightened by the author's rigid justice to her; she is not caricatured by a light or a shadow, and her dim sense of Theobald's goodness and purity is even flattered into prominence. In all essentials one has from this story the solid satisfaction given by work in which the conception is fine, and the expression nowhere falls below it—if we except one point that seems to us rather essential, in a thing so carefully tempered and closely wrought. The reiteration of the Italian figure-maker's philosophy, "Cats and monkeys, monkeys and cats; all human life is there," is apparently of but wandering purport, and to end the pensive strain of the romance with it is to strike a jarring note that leaves the reader's mind out of tune. Sometimes even the ladies and gentlemen of Mr. James's stories are allowed a certain excess or violence in which the end to be achieved is not distinctly discernible, or the effect so reluctantly responds to the intention as to leave merely the sense of the excess.

Eugene Pickering is, like Madame de Mauves, one of those realistic subjects which we find less real than the author's romantic inspirations. There is no fault with the treatment; that is thoroughly admirable, full of spirit, wit, and strength; but there is a fancifulness in the outlines of Pickering's history and the fact of his strange betrothal which seems to belong to an old-fashioned stage-play method of fiction rather than to such a modern affair as that between the unsophisticated American and Madame Blumenthal; it did not need that machinery to produce this effect, thanks to common conditions of ours that often enough keep young men as guileless as Pickering, and as fit for sacrifice at such shrines as hers. However, something must always be granted to the story-teller by way of premises; if we exacted from Mr. James only that he should make his premises fascinating, we should have nothing to ask here. His start, in fact, is always superb; he possesses himself of your interest at once, and he never relinquishes it till the end; though there he may sometimes leave your curiosity not quite satisfied on points such as a story-teller assumes to make clear. What, for example, were exactly the tortuous workings of Madame Blumenthal's mind in her self-contradictory behavior towards Pickering? These things must be at least unmistakably suggested.

Since Hawthorne's Donatello, any attempt to touch what seems to be the remaining paganism in Italian character must accuse itself a little, but The Last of the Valerii is a study of this sort that need really have nothing on its conscience. It is an eminently poetic conceit, though it appeals to a lighter sort of emotions than any other story in Mr. James's book; it is an airy fabric woven from those bewitching glimpses of the impossible which life in Italy affords, and which those who have enjoyed them are perfectly right to overvalue. It has just the right tint of ideal trouble in it which no living writer could have imparted more skillfully than it is here done. If the story is of slighter material than the others, the subtlety of its texture gives it a surpassing charm and makes it worthy to be named along with the only other purely romantic tale in the book.

To our thinking, Mr. James has been conspicuously fortunate in placing his Romance of Certain Old Clothes in that eighteenth-century New England when the country, still colonial, was no longer rigidly puritanic, and when a love of splendor and accumulating wealth had created social conditions very different from those conventionally attributed to New England. It is among such bravely dressing provincials as Copley used to paint, and as dwelt in fine town mansions in Boston, or the handsome country-places which still remember their faded grandeur along Brattle Street in Cambridge, that Mr. James finds the circumstance and material of his personages; and we greatly enjoy the novelty of this conception of what not only might, but must have existed hereabouts in times which we are too prone to fancy all close-cropped and sad-colored. The tale is written with heat, and rapidly advances from point to point, with a constantly mounting interest. The sisterly rivalry is shown with due boldness, but without excess, and the character of Viola is sketched with a vigor that conveys a full sense of her selfish, luxurious beauty. The scene between her and Perdita when the engagement of the latter is betrayed, the scene in which she unrolls the stuff of the wedding-dress and confronts herself in the glass with it falling from her shoulder, and that in which she hastily tries the garment on after her sister's marriage, are pictures as full of character as they are of color. The most is made of Perdita where she lies dying, and bids her husband keep her fine clothes for her little girl; it is very affecting indeed, and all the more so for the explicit human-nature of the dying wife's foreboding. In the whole course of the story nothing is urged, nothing is dwelt upon; and all our story-tellers, including Mr. James himself, could profitably take a lesson from it in this respect. At other times he has a tendency to expatiate upon his characters too much, and not to trust his reader's perception enough. For the sake of a more dramatic presentation of his persons, he has told most of the stories in this book as things falling within the notice of the assumed narrator; an excellent device; though it would be better if the assumed narrator were able to keep himself from seeming to patronize the simpler-hearted heroes, and from openly rising above them in a worldly way.

But this is a very little matter, and none of our discontents with Mr. James bear any comparison to the pleasure we have had in here renewing our acquaintance with stories as distinctly characteristic as anything in literature. It is indeed a marvelous first book in which the author can invite his critic to the same sort of reflection that criticism bestows upon the claims of the great reputations; but one cannot dismiss this volume with less and not slight it. Like it or not, you must own that here is something positive, original, individual, the result of long and studious effort in a well-considered line, and mounting in its own way to great achievement. We have a reproachful sense of leaving the immense suggestiveness of the book scarcely touched, and we must ask the reader to supply our default from the stories themselves. He may be assured that nothing more novel in our literature has yet fallen in his way; and we are certain that he will not close the book without a lively sense of its force. We can promise him, also, his own perplexities about it, among which may be a whimsical doubt whether Mr. James has not too habitually addressed himself less to men and women in their mere humanity, than to a certain kind of cultivated people, who, well as they are in some ways, and indispensable as their appreciation is, are often a little narrow in their sympathies and poverty-stricken in the simple emotions; who are so, or try to be so, which is quite as bad, or worse.

TRANSATLANTIC SKETCHES*

—As there is no common ground whereon those who have traveled and those who have not can meet to compare their impressions regarding the things which, even unseen, are eternal in every one's consciousness, it is impossible to say to which class of readers Mr. James's records and reminiscences of England, Germany, Switzerland, the Low Countries, and Italy will give most enjoyment; whether they have more power to suggest or to recall. In either case the satisfaction will be so full and so peculiar that each class will feel there is nothing to envy the other. Mr. James's mode of writing travels is unusual: he gives us no history, no legends; quotes no poetry; tells no personal adventures, or very few; what he treats of are the external aspects and "the soul of things," to use an expression of his own: but all that he tells of what he sees, detects, or divines, is saturated with the essence of a penetrating individuality. In his method, perhaps, he has taken a lesson from the French writers on foreign lands, with Théophile Gautier at their head, but it is the eye and brain of an American which he brings to bear on the subjects of his observation. He is a triumphant and most comfortable proof—to such of us as have been troubled by doubts on the question—that a high, perhaps the highest, degree of general culture, drawn as it must ever be from the old imperishable springs, in nowise impairs the natural character of real talent. He never obtrudes his information, but it en-

* *Atlantic Monthly* (July, 1875).

riches every line that he writes. In England two impressions are always being made upon his mind: that of the outward, actual, and present, and one reflected from these but refracted from the mirror of the past,—from the humorists of the last century, the novelists of fifty years ago, the poets and dramatists of Elizabethan and earlier times. His article on the Parisian theatres is seasoned by familiarity with the French drama, the traditions of the stage in that and other countries, the long habit of intelligent play-going, and the fine critical discernment which admits no confusion between the merit of the pieces and the actor, the school and individual genius. Wherever he goes, he looks at pictures, statues, buildings, with the eye of a connoisseur, and at nature with the gaze of an artist and a worshiper. For if a round tower in the distance, or a pillared portico in the foreground of a landscape, together with certain circumstances of earth and sky, make it to him less a simple view than a picture by Claude, his sense is as keen for the beauty of a wood-bank covered with wild flowers, "in the raw green light of early spring,"—a subject no painter has yet attempted with success.

Nobody has so fully conveyed as Mr. James the peculiar feelings of an American in Europe: the mingled pain and happiness we feel in England, as of coming to our own at last, yet finding ourselves aliens and exiles there (for let no American think of it as home; we do not and cannot belong to it, nor it to us); the blissful, unquestioning, "irresponsible" (to use his favorite word) relaxation of that terrible tension in which we live here, which comes to us in Italy; the sense of history in the very air of the Old World, so unrecognized by most Europeans, so sensible to us in every breath we draw there; the sudden revelation of the picturesque, "the crooked, the accidental, the unforeseen, . . . the architectural surprises, caprices, and fantasies, . . . the infinite accident and infinite effect which give a wholly novel zest to the use of the eyes," and gradually produce a boundless expansion of the range of perception. Nobody else has so faithfully and minutely described the various stages and phases of our acquaintance with foreign parts, from the excitement of first visits to the deep delight of return, the rapturous unrest of novelty, the rapturous repose of familiarity. He has too the faculty of hitting the peculiarity which makes foreigners seem odd to us, but which we are at a loss ourselves to define, so that when he speaks of traveling English people, for instance, we think he must have met the very lady who sat beside us at the *table d'hôte* at Interlaken, or the gentleman with whom we went through the Mont Cenis tunnel. He moralizes and philosophizes very casually; he writes with the careless indulgence of one who is only in quest of enjoyment, and who finds it on all sides; yet here and there a chance remark probes national failings sharp and deep. Mr. James has the profound, romantic enthusiasm for England which only an American can feel, and he has it in perfection; yet he gauges her pretensions with a steady hand. "Conservatism here has all the charm, and leaves dissent and democracy and other vulgar variations, nothing but their bald logic. Conservatism has the cathedrals, the colleges, the castles, the gardens, the traditions, the associations, the fine names, the better manners, the poetry. Dissent has the dusty brick chapels in provincial by-streets, the names out of Dickens, the uncertain tenure of the *h*, and the poor *mens sibi conscia recti*. Differences which in other countries are slight and varying, almost metaphysical, as one may say, are marked in England by a gulf. Nowhere does the degree of one's respectability involve such solid consequences." And again: "The bishop sat facing me, enthroned in a stately Gothic alcove, and clad in his crimson bands, his lawn sleeves, and his lavender gloves; the canons in their degree with the arch-deacons, as I suppose, reclined comfortably in the carven stalls, and the scanty congregation fringed the broad aisle. But though scanty, the congregation was select; it was unexceptionably black-coated, bonneted, and gloved. It savored intensely, in short, of that inexorable gentility which the English put on with their Sunday bonnets and beavers, and which fills me—as a purely sentimental tourist—with a sort of fond reactionary remembrance of those animated bundles of rags which one sees kneeling in the churches in Italy." Now Italy is the country for which Mr. James cherishes and confesses an incurable weakness; Germany, despite the pretty touches in his chapters on Homburg and Darmstadt, is, we suspect, a land to which it costs him nothing to deal the sternest justice; yet a fortnight after leaving the Lake of Como for Hesse, he writes, "I have shifted my standard of beauty, but it still commands a glimpse of the divine idea. There is something here too which pleases, suggests, and satisfies. Sitting of an evening in the Kurgarten, within ear-shot of the music, you have an almost inspiring feeling that you never have in Italy; a feeling that the substantial influences about you are an element of the mysterious future. They are of that varied order which seems to indicate the large needs of large natures."

As yet we have not spoken of what, after all, is the chief charm, the spell, of Mr. James's style—a felicity of epithets, an exquisite choice and use of language, a graphic and pictorial quality in his mere words, which impart to his description that property which every one has felt in a scent, a sound, or a hue, to awaken the memory of impressions and sensations, to revive the very reality of a vanished moment. Not the scene alone is before your eyes, you are conscious of the atmosphere of the place and time, and the emotions with which you were filled. But this gift sometimes betrays its possessor into an abuse. There is danger of his over-refining his expressions, of overloading his phrases with adverbs and adjectives. He has a large vocabulary for the finer, more delicate, subtle, and evanescent or impalpable shades of difference, whether in the material or in the supersensuous order, but they are terms whose expressiveness and effectiveness depend a good deal on their being used sparingly; so he should beware of the pleasure of having pet words and phrases. The fault is more than skin-deep, too, though we fancy the origin was on the surface and that it has struck in rather than come out; for there is a tendency to distill and subtilize the thought, or simile, which he recognizes when he catches himself "spinning his fancies rather too fine." He is over fond of the triple extract of an idea. To this same error of taste appears to belong an occasional trick of letting you down suddenly from a highly poetic fancy to a cynical or common-place conclusion, a habit which in Mr. James may be ascribed to the influence of Hawthorne, who carried it to a point which was almost intolerable. But the risk of becoming a sort of *petit maître* of style, a metaphysical euphuist, is much more imminent. One who has read his papers singly, at intervals, with almost unalloyed pleasure, cannot help wondering with some dread what the effect would be, in going through the volume, of a number of such sentences as the following: The wood-carving in Siena cathedral "is like the frost-work on one's window-panes interpreted in polished oak." We fear it would beget a gnawing hunger for the daily bread of common speech. But it must not be inferred that all the virtue of his descriptive power lies in these superfine touches, or even his extraordinary command of color; he has a bold, graphic way of putting a picture before you in a few strokes of black and white: "Florence lay amid her checkered fields and gardens, with as many towers and spires as a chess-board half cleared."

It would be no injustice to Mr. James or his publishers, if space allowed, to quote half a hundred of his most charming passages. To make an extract from the Italian sketches is most difficult; they are a study, or an enjoyment, apart, and should be read as a separate series. Exquisitely as Mr. James writes about England, charming and playful and true as are his chapters on other countries, it is only Italy that calls forth his full poetic power; we choose the following description of the Protestant cemetery at Rome, partly because it has been so often described before: "Here is a mixture of tears and smiles, of stones and flowers, of mourning cypresses and radiant sky, which almost tempts one to fancy one is looking back at death from the brighter side of the grave. The cemetery nestles in an angle of the city wall, and the older graves are sheltered by a mass of ancient brick-work, through whose narrow loop-holes you may peep at the purple landscape of the Campagna. Shelley's grave is here, buried in roses—a happy grave every way for a poet who was personally poetic. It is impossible to imagine anything more impenetrably tranquil than this little corner in the bend of the protecting rampart. You seem to see a cluster of modern ashes held tenderly in the rugged hand of the Past."

FRENCH POETS AND NOVELISTS*

If novelists and poets are not the best critics of their art, they are often the most suggestive commentators upon it; and when they have the skill to formulate and weave together their opinions they give us something rather better than mere criticism. Readers of Mr. Henry James, Jr., were for some time, and a few of them may still be, in doubt whether he is more a novelist than critic; but we think his recent volume of essays may go a good way towards fixing the opinion that his peculiar attractiveness in this line of writing is due in great measure to the fact that he is himself a creative artist. His reviews of other writers are not precisely criticism, but they possess a pleasant flavor of criticism, agreeably diffused through a mass of sympathetic and often keenly analytical impressions. It is saying a great deal when we admit that he reminds us more of Sainte-Beuve than any other English writer; but he is more a *causeur* than the author of the famous Causeries, and less a critic in the systematic sense. We hardly know how we can fully illustrate our meaning except by more references and quotations than it is convenient to make here. But let the reader turn to the splendid chapter on Balzac, who has never before received so abundant and interesting a showing, within similar compass, as at Mr. James's hands. In this there are to be found most of the interesting facts of Balzac's life grouped with good judgment, a sketchy view of the character of his works, and a great many

* *Atlantic Monthly* (July, 1878).

vivid statements of the impressions produced by them. But we can imagine that to a person who had read nothing of Balzac the article would have an exasperating inconclusiveness. It is a mixture of the frankest admiration and (to use Mr. James's own word) of brutal snubbing, which continues to the very last page. The one unqualified statement—and that, by the way, is a real gain to one's stock of well-defined perceptions—is that Balzac's great characteristic was his "sense of this present terrestrial life, which has never been surpassed, and in which his genius overshadowed everything else." For the rest, we are given to understand that his greatest merits were his greatest faults; that his novels are ponderous and shapeless, yet have more composition and more grasp on the reader's attention than any others, etc. "He believed that he was about as creative as the Deity, and that if mankind and human history were swept away the Comédie Humaine would be a perfectly adequate substitute for them," is the writer's witty statement of the degree of his conceit; and he quotes Taine, approvingly, as saying that after Shakespeare Balzac is our great magazine of documents on human nature; yet this he partially retracts, again, by saying that when Shakespeare is suggested we feel rather Balzac's differences from him. The French novelist's atmosphere, we are told, is musty, limited, artificial. In the next sentence, however, Mr. James assures us that, notwithstanding this "artificial" atmosphere, Balzac is to be taken, like Shakespeare, as a final authority on human nature. Then again he lowers him a peg by saying that he lacked "that slight but needful thing,—charm." "But our last word about him is that he had incomparable power." The writer himself seems to feel, in this closing sentence, that he has given a somewhat too paradoxical summary. The same difficulty could be raised with all the other essays in this collection, excepting the one on Tourguéneff, which comes near being a masterpiece of criticism, and perhaps ought to be decidedly rated as such. In general, there is a want of some positive or negative result clearly enunciated; and the presence of such results is what, to our mind, distinguishes the systematic critic like Sainte-Beuve or Matthew Arnold from the highly suggestive, charming talker like Mr. James.

If we are speaking of criticism, the question is whether we are to approach as nearly as possible to an equation of conflicting views, or whether we are to work out a problem to some conclusion on one side or the other. As a matter of definition we are inclined to say that pure criticism has for its aim the latter task. In the case of Balzac, for example, there is a wonderful stimulus and surprise in the obvious inadequacy and disrelish with which Sainte-Beuve treats him. The very narrowness of his judgment has a value. Mr. James may say that he does not write either for readers who simply want information about French authors, or for those who prefer opinions that cut only one way; and that he cultivates breadth, of set purpose. It is not necessary, however, to be narrow in taking a side: there are critics who show the finest comprehension of all the aspects of a genius, yet on the whole advocate a certain view with satisfactory unity and consecutiveness. We find fault with Mr. James's attitude, judged as a critic, because it implies a certain nervousness that if he curtails his contradictory impressions he may not appear liberal enough. With less extreme expression and more art, liberality need not fear to be overlooked. A fault connected with this is the tone of patronage which the writer is led to take towards the larger minds among those which he discusses; and possibly attributable to the same source is a not altogether pleasant jocularity in the treatment of those dubious relations between men and women which the themes selected naturally involve.

But we have said that a creative artist discoursing on the works of other creators can be more entertaining than the mere critic; and Mr. James is irresistible in the ease and brilliancy of his style, and the felicity with which he calls our attention to the qualities most to be admired in his subjects and traces some of the reasons why they are admirable. Next to the Tourguéneff we like best the paper on De Musset, which differs from all the others in having to some extent the tone of advocacy, and pushing its view of the poet with a thoroughly enjoyable ardor. That on Mérimée's Letters is almost too slight to keep company with the rest, and we do not know how to excuse, in the essay on the Théatre Français, the haste with which Mlle. Sarah Bernhard is passed by. Even with the style, too, one is occasionally dissatisfied, owing to some obscurity which seems to be due to a disinclination to correct. It is regrettable that we have not space to pay the homage of quotation to several of the searching, the humorous, the sympathetic things which Mr. James scatters copiously over his pages; and we cannot deny ourselves, in closing, the privilege of reproducing here, if only in tribute to our own appreciativeness, these fragments from the shrewd and trenchant essay on Baudelaire. "A good way to embrace Baudelaire at a glance is to say that he was in his treatment of evil exactly what Hawthorne was not,—Hawthorne, who felt the thing at its source, deep in the human consciousness. Baudelaire's infinitely slighter genius apart, he was a sort of Hawthorne reversed." "The crudity of sentiment of the advocates of 'art for art' is often a striking example of the fact that a great deal of what is called culture may fail to dissipate a well-seated provincialism of spirit. They talk of morality as Miss Edgeworth's infantine heroes and heroines talk of 'physic'. . . It is in reality simply a part of the essential richness of inspiration,—it has nothing to do with the artistic process, and it has everything to do with the artistic effect." That is almost the best thing in this superior book. The point has hardly been put with so much grasp and cleverness before.

DAISY MILLER AND THE EUROPEANS*

—I read Avis, and gave thanks. Its feverish intensity and occasionally vicious rhetoric did not escape me, but the brave, clear intent of the book was so all-engrossing to me, as to the author, that I was utterly bewildered by the hue and cry of the critics. Dare I confess it? Even yet I am not quite convinced that this book (of which I had said in my crass ignorance, "If ever I know a young man and maid, worth saving, to be betrothed, I will present each of them with Avis, that they may see how sacred a thing is holy matrimony; 'not to be by any enterprised nor taken in hand unadvisedly, lightly, or wantonly,' as the English service has it") bristles with hatred of marriage *per se*, disdain of homely duties, and all the other ugly appurtenances of a presumedly "woman's rights" creation—not quite convinced, I say, that these discoveries in Miss Phelps's book are not wholly evolved from the minds of the critics.

So, in regard to Mr. Henry James's Daisy Miller, I am shocked to find that what I gratefully accepted as an exquisitely loyal service to American girlhood abroad is regarded by some critical experts as "servilely snobbish" and "brutally unpatriotic."

Nevertheless, whenever Mr. James has occasion for a monument, which, however, I devoutly hope may not be while my reading-lamp holds out to burn, I will contribute my humble

* "The Contributor's Club," *Atlantic Monthly* (February, 1879).

share towards perpetuating the memory of this valiant champion (faithful among the faithless found) of the young American What-is-it, whose beauty and whose vagaries are the eighth wonder of the other hemisphere.

—Mr. James calls his short tale, Daisy Miller, recently published in the Cornhill and the Living Age, a study. His longer story of The Europeans is a collection of portraits of character carefully studied. It is perfect work of its kind, and delightful reading to those whom such study interests. There is great satisfaction in seeing a thing well done, and both in the substance and in the style of his books Mr. James always offers an intellectual treat to appreciative readers; of course it is obvious that he writes only for the cultivated minority. But among his admirers are many who complain of him as a disappointing author,—one who charms their interest from the first, and keeps it alive to the end, but who, at the end, is apt to leave them somewhat dissatisfied. The conclusions of his novels and tales, they say, seem to them a breaking off rather than a true finishing of the lives and fortunes of the personages he has made them acquainted with. He gives reality and vitality to his characters only to make the reader close the book, asking, Is that all about them? It is not enough, or not the end they should come to. This is a reproach, it seems to me, applicable to many weaker authors, less skilled in their art, but not to Mr. James. In his case the apparent failure to come to anything particular is foreseen by the author himself, because it is inherent in the nature of the theme chosen. It is certainly evident that the author of Roderick Hudson and The American has not the genuine story-telling gift, the power of inventing a story interesting for its own sake. His talent lies in another field, that of keen observation and fine discrimination of character, which he portrays with a subtle and delicate touch. It is unreasonable, I think, to complain of a writer for not being something else than he is, as it would be to find fault with a figure painter that he was not a landscape artist. When we have once recognized the quality of a man's talent, why not take what he can give, and not ask for something different? Let us do without a story in Mr. James's novels, and enjoy instead something certainly as admirable in its way. Observing the refined skill with which the contrast of typical characters is presented in The Europeans, I, for one, was not disposed to demand a more exciting *dénoûment*, the interest of each page as I read it being pleasure sufficient.

DEFENSE OF DAISY MILLER*

—To read the silly criticisms which have been printed, and the far sillier ones which are every day uttered in regard to Mr. James's Daisy Miller would almost convince us that we are as provincial as ever in our sensitiveness to foreign opinion. It is actually regarded as a species of unpardonable incivism for Mr. James, because he lives in London, to describe an under-bred American family traveling in Europe. The fact that he has done so with a touch of marvelous delicacy and truth, that he has produced not so much a picture as a photograph, is held by many to be an aggravating circumstance. Only the most shiveringly sensitive of our shoddy population are bold enough to deny the truth of this wonderful little sketch. To those best acquainted with Mr. James's manner (and I believe I have read every word he has printed) Daisy Miller was positively startling in its straightforward simplicity and what I can only call *authenticity.* It could not have been written—I am almost ready to say it cannot be appreciated—except by one who has lived so long abroad as to be able to look at his own people with the eyes of a foreigner. All poor Daisy's crimes are purely conventional. She is innocent and good at heart, susceptible of praise and blame; she does not wish even to surprise, much less outrage, the stiffest of her censors. In short, the things she does with such dire effect at Vevay and at Rome would never for an instant be remarked or criticised in

* "The Contributor's Club," *Atlantic Monthly* (March, 1879).

Schenectady. They would provoke no comment in Buffalo or Cleveland; they would be a matter of course in Richmond and Louisville. One of the most successful touches in the story is that where Daisy, astonished at being cut by American ladies, honestly avows her disbelief in their disapproval. "I should not think you would let them be so unkind!" she cries to Winterbourne, conscious of her innocence, and bewildered at the cruelty of a sophisticated world. Yet with such exquisite art is this study managed that the innocence and loveliness of Miss Miller are hardly admitted as extenuating circumstances in her reprehensible course of conduct. She is represented, by a chronicler who loves and admires her, as bringing ruin upon herself and a certain degree of discredit upon her country-women, through eccentricities of behavior for which she cannot justly be held responsible. Her conduct is without blemish, according to the rural American standard, and she knows no other. It is the merest ignorance or affectation, on the part of the anglicized Americans of Boston or New York, to deny this. A few dozens, perhaps a few hundreds, of families in America have accepted the European theory of the necessity of surveillance for young ladies, but it is idle to say it has ever been accepted by the country at large. In every city of the nation young girls of good family, good breeding, and perfect innocence of heart and mind, receive their male acquaintances *en tête-à-tête*, and go to parties and concerts with them, unchaperoned. Of course, I do not mean that Daisy Miller belongs to that category; her astonishing mother at once designates her as pertaining to one distinctly inferior. Who has not met them abroad? From the first word uttered by Miss Daisy to her rampant young brother in the garden at Vevay, "Well, I guess you'd better be quiet," you recognize her, and recall her under a dozen different names and forms. She went to dine with you one day at Sceaux, and climbed, with the fearless innocence of a bird, into the great chestnut-tree. She challenged you to take her to Schönbrunn, and amazed your Austrian acquaintances whom you met there, and who knew you were not married. At Naples, one evening—*Eheu, fugaces labuntur anni;* it is not worth while to continue the enumeration. It makes you feel melancholy to think she is doing the same acts of innocent recklessness with men as young and as happy, and what the French call as unenterprising, as you were once.

As to the usefulness of this little book, it seems to me as indubitable as its literary excellence. It is too long a question to discuss in this place, whether the freedom of American girls at home is beneficial or sinister in its results. But there is no question whatever as to the effect of their ignorance or defiance of conventionalities abroad. An innocent flirtation with a Frenchman or Italian tarnishes a reputation forever. All the waters of the Mediterranean cannot wash clean the name of a young lady who makes a rendezvous and takes a walk with a fascinating chance acquaintance. We need only refer to the darker miseries which often result from these reckless intimacies. A charming young girl, traveling with a simple-minded mother, a few years ago, in a European capital, married a branded convict who had introduced himself to them, calling himself, of course, a count. In short, an American girl, like Daisy Miller, accompanied by a woman like Daisy's mother, brought up in the simplicity of provincial life in the United States, has no more chance of going through Europe unscathed in her feelings and her character than an idiot millionaire has of amusing himself economically in Wall Street. This lesson is taught in Mr. James's story,—and never was necessary medicine administered in a form more delightful and unobtrusive.

The intimacy with the courier is a fact of daily observation on the Continent. A gentleman of my acquaintance, inquiring the other day for a courier he had employed some years before, was told that he was spoiled for any reasonable service by having been so much with American families, and that one family, after their tour in Europe was ended, had taken him home to South Boston as their guest, and had given a party for him!

JAMES'S HAWTHORNE*

Mr. James's book on Hawthorne, in Morley's English Men of Letters series, merits far closer examination and carefuller notice than we can give it here, alike for the interest of its subject, the peculiarity of its point of view, and the charm and distinction of its literature. An American author writing of an American author for an English public incurs risks with his fellow-countrymen which Mr. James must have faced, and is much more likely to possess the foreigner whom he addresses with a clear idea of our conditions than to please the civilization whose portrait is taken. Forty-six, fifty, sixty-four, are not dates so remote, nor are Salem and Concord societies so extinct, that the people of those periods and places can be safely described as provincial, not once, but a dozen times; and we foresee, without any very powerful prophetic lens, that Mr. James will be in some quarters promptly attainted of high treason. For ourselves, we will be content with saying that the provinciality strikes us as somewhat over-insisted upon, and that, speaking from the point of not being at all provincial ourselves, we think the epithet is sometimes mistaken. If it is not provincial for an Englishman to be English or a Frenchman French, then it is not so for an American to be American; and if Hawthorne was "exquisitely provincial," one had better take one's chance of universality with him than with almost any Londoner or Parisian of his time. Provinciality, we understand

* *The Atlantic Monthly* (February, 1880).

it, is a thing of the mind or the soul; but if it is a thing of the experiences, then that is another matter, and there is no quarrel. Hawthorne undoubtedly saw less of the world in New England than one sees in Europe, but he was no cockney, as Europeans are apt to be.

At the same time we must not be thought to deny the value and delightfulness of those chapters on Salem and Brook Farm and Concord. They are not very close in description, and the places seem deliciously divined rather than studied. But where they are used unjustly, there will doubtless be abundant defense; and if Salem or Brook Farm be mute, the welkin will probably respond to the cries of certain critics who lie in wait to make life sorrowful to any one dealing lightly with the memory of Thoreau or the presence of the poet Channing. What will happen to a writer who says of the former that he was "worse than provincial, he was parochial," and of the latter that he resembled the former in "having produced literary compositions more esteemed by the few than by the many," we wait with the patience and security of a spectator at an *auto da fé,* to see. But even an unimbattled outsider may suggest that the essential large-mindedness of Concord, as expressed in literature, is not sufficiently recognized, although it is thoroughly felt. The treatment of the culture foible and of the colorless aesthetic joys, the attribution of "a great deal of Concord five and thirty years ago" to the remark of a visitor of Hawthorne that Margaret Fuller "had risen perceptibly into a higher state of being since their last meeting," are exquisite,— too exquisite, we fear, for the sense of most Englishmen, and not too fine only for the rarefied local consciousness which they may sting. Emerson is indeed devoutly and amply honored, and there is something particularly sweet and tender in the characterization of such surviving Brook Farmers as the author remembers to have met; but even in speaking of Emerson, Mr. James has the real misfortune to call his grand poem for the dedication of the monument to Concord Fight a "little hymn." It is little as Milton's sonnet on Shakespeare is little.

We think, too, that in his conscience against brag and *chauvinism* Mr. James puts too slight a value upon some of Hawthorne's work. It is not enough to say of a book so wholly unexampled and unrivaled as The Scarlet Letter that it was "the finest piece of imaginative writing put forth in" America; as if it had its parallel in any literature. When he comes to speak of the romance in detail, he repairs this defect of estimation in some degree; but here again his strictures seem somewhat mistaken. No one better than Mr. James knows the radical difference between a romance and a novel, but he speaks now of Hawthorne's novels, and now of his romances, throughout, as if the terms were convertible; whereas the romance and the novel are as distinct as the poem and the novel. Mr. James excepts to the people in The Scarlet Letter, because they are rather types than persons, rather conditions of the mind than characters; as if it were not almost precisely the business of the romance to deal with types and mental conditions. Hawthorne's fictions being always and essentially, in conception and performance, romances, and not novels, something of all Mr. James's special criticism is invalidated by the confusion which, for some reason not made clear, he permits himself. Nevertheless, his analysis of the several books and of the shorter tales is most interesting; and though we should ourselves place The Blithedale Romance before The House of the Seven Gables, and should rank it much higher than Mr. James seems to do, we find ourselves consenting oftener than dissenting as we read his judgments. An admirably clear and just piece of criticism, we think, is that in which he pronounces upon the slighter and cheaper *motif* of Septimius Felton. But here there are not grounds for final sentence; it is possible, if that book had received the author's last touches, it might have been, after all, a playful and gentle piece of irony rather than a tragedy.

What gives us entire satisfaction, however, is Mr. James's characterization, or illustration, of Hawthorne's own nature. He finds him an innocent, affectionate heart, extremely domestic, a life definite, high purposes singularly unbaffled, and an "unperplexed intellect." The black problem of evil, with which his Puritan ancestors wrestled concretely, in groans and despair, and which darkens with its portentous shadow nearly everything that Hawthorne wrote, has become his literary material; or, in Mr. James's finer and more luminous phrase, he "transmutes this heavy moral burden into the very substance of the imagination." This strikes us as beautifully reasonable and true, and we will not cloud it with comment of ours. But satisfactorily as Mr. James declares Hawthorne's personality in large, we do not find him sufficient as to minor details and facts. His defect, or his error, appears oftenest in his discussion of the note-books, where he makes plain to himself the simple, domestic, democratic qualities in Hawthorne, and yet maintains that he sets down slight and little aspects of nature because his world is small and vacant. Hawthorne noted these because he loved them, and as a great painter, however full and vast his world is, continues to jot down whatever strikes him as picturesque and characteristic. The disposition to allege this inadequate reason comes partly from that confusion of the novelist's and the romancer's work of which we have spoken, and partly from a theory, boldly propounded, that it needs a long history and "a complex social machinery to set a writer in motion." Hawthorne himself shared, or seemed to share, this illusion, and wrote The Marble Faun, so inferior, with its foreign scene, to the New England romances, to prove the absurdity of it. As a romancer, the twelve years of boyhood which he spent in the wild solitudes of Maine were probably of greater advantage to him than if they had been passed at Eton and Oxford. At least, until some other civilization has produced a romantic genius at all comparable to his, we must believe this. After leaving out all those novelistic "properties," as sovereigns, courts, aristocracy, gentry, castles, cottages, cathedrals, abbeys, universities, museums, political class, Epsoms, and Ascots, by the absence of which Mr. James suggests our poverty to the English conception, we have the whole of human life remaining, and a social structure presenting the only fresh and novel opportunities left to fiction, opportunities manifold and inexhaustible. No man would have known less what to do with that dreary and worn-out paraphernalia than Hawthorne.

We can only speak of the excellent comment upon Hawthorne's Old Home, and the skillful and manly way in which Mr. James treats of that delicate subject to his English audience. Skillful and manly the whole book is,—a miracle of tact and of self-respect, which the author need not fear to trust to the best of either of his publics. There is nothing to regret in the attitude of the book; and its literature is always a high pleasure, scarcely marred by some evidences of hurry, and such *writerish* passages as that in which *sin* is spoken of as "this baleful substantive with its attendant adjective."

It is a delightful and excellent essay, refined and delicate in perception, generous in feeling, and a worthy study of the unique romancer whom its closing words present with justice so subtle and expression so rich:—

"He was a beautiful, natural, original genius, and his life had been singularly exempt from worldly preoccupations and vulgar efforts. It had been as pure, as simple, as unsophisticated, as his work. He had lived primarily in his domestic affections, which were of the tenderest kind; and then—without eagerness, without pretension, but with a great deal of quiet devotion—in his charming art. His work will remain; it is too original and exquisite to pass away; among the men of imagination he will always have his niche. No one has had just that vision of life, and no one has had a literary form that more successfully expressed his vision. He was not a moralist, and he was not simply a poet. The moralists are weightier, denser, richer, in a sense; the poets are more purely inconclusive and irresponsible. He combined in a singular degree the spontaneity of the imagination with a haunting care for moral problems. Man's conscience was his theme, but he saw it in the light of a creative fancy which added, out of its own substance, an interest, and, I may almost say, an importance."

PART TWO

Articles and Reviews of

1881-1888

INTRODUCTION

In 1881 Howells left his position as editor-in-chief of the *Atlantic* to devote himself to writing and from 1882 to 1890 he published ten volumes; among them were *A Modern Instance* (1882), *The Rise of Silas Lapham* (1885), *Indian Summer* (1886), and *Annie Kilburn* (1888). During this same period James published fifteen books; and among these were *Confidence* (1880), *Washington Square* (1881), *Portrait of a Lady* (1881), *The Bostonians* (1886) and *The Princess Casimassima* (1886). Howells reviewed only *The Princess Casimassima,* the stories reprinted in *The Aspern Papers* and *A London Life,* and *The Reverberator.* He did, however, publish in 1882 his highly provocative "Henry James, Jr."; and James reciprocated by writing his inclusive review of Howells' works which was published in June, 1886, in *Harper's Weekly.*[1]

In the fall of 1881 James, who had resided in Europe since the autumn of 1875, returned to the United States. On January 29, 1882, his mother died after seemingly having recovered from, as he described it, "an attack of bronchial asthma." When Howells wrote to John Hay on March 18, 1882, he remarked that James and his three brothers had "carried their mother to her grave" and that, as James had related the incident to him, it was "most touching." To Howells, Henry James—who was "spending the winter only a few doors" away —had not "sensibly changed"—nor, he added, had he himself as he saw himself "reflected in" his friend. Howells remarked that he and James saw each other constantly and talked "literature perpetually"—just as they had done in their "walks ten years ago." He stated also that James had intended to return to England in April but that this plan had been "broken up by the sudden death of his mother." He doubted that James would "stay continually abroad again while his father lives."

In May, 1882, James returned to England; and Howells and his family left in July for Quebec and sailed from there to England to begin the year abroad which, they hoped, would provide literary material for Howells and health for his daughter Winifred, who had been ill. James had secured for Howells a "very charming lodging" in South Kensington; and there he visited his friend. James did all he could to make the sojourn abroad a happy one; it was already an exhilarating one, for Howells realized for the first time the full extent of his international popularity and reputation.

In August, 1882, Howells wrote James R. Osgood, his publisher, that James had been very kind and that, not wanting to do any writing at the moment, he had rejected an offer for a story from Thomas Bailey Aldrich. During this month Howells and James must have discussed "Henry James, Jr.," the article Howells was writing for the *Century*. Since Howells had read before publication James's review of his poetry, it is also more than probable that James read the article before it appeared in November, 1882.

In this review of James's life, literary career, and artistic superiority, Howells stated that "the art of fiction has . . . become a finer art in our day than it was with Dickens and Thackeray." He also averred that "we could not suffer the confidential attitude of" Thackeray "now, nor the manner of" Dickens "any more than we could endure the prolixity of Richardson or the coarseness of Fielding." He also classified Reade and Trollope as writers of the past and declared that the "new school derives from Hawthorne and George Eliot" in its study of human motivations and was "largely influenced by French fiction in form."

Although Howells' comments seem commonplace to us today, his remarks about the new fiction and the artistry of English novelists were considered sheer insolence in 1882 and aroused, therefore, a furor. The Howells who had been famous in London now became not only infamous but the center of attack by the English quarterlies and newspapers. The writer in the *Quarterly Review* of January, 1883, labeled Howells and James as "Transatlantic aesthetic reformers" who were "dull, unspeakably dull." Although Howells from the moment of the first reaction was dismayed by the attack, he wrote Roswell Smith of the *Century* that he was willing to amplify and intensify his views for he knew what he was writing about and his critics did not.

During this onslaught of unfavorable criticism which was launched against Howells and James in the United States as well as in England, James was in his own country; he returned home in December, 1882, because of his father's approaching death. On July 30, 1883, Howells, now back in Boston, wrote to John Hay about James's paper about Charles Dudley Warner, who had opposed the theory of realism: "I haven't yet read all of James's paper, but what he said of Warner's theory of fiction was all gospel."

In August, 1883, James returned to England; and on August 22, 1884, Howells wrote him from Kennebunkport, Maine, to express his reactions to James's "A New England Winter," a tale which James included in *Tales of Three Cities* (1884) but not—despite Howells' laudatory comments—in his New York Edition. To Howells this creation—which was creating a favorable impression among the "well-dressed and well-read girls" and which was influencing "the female Boston mind with a firm resolve to walk on the domestic roof at the first opportunity"—contained some particularly excellent "bits of painting" and "fine touches by which" James suggested "a more artistically difficult and evasive Boston" than Howells could, as he confessed, "get at." James, wrote Howells, captured the fashionableness of Boston which was so distinguished from that quality of other cities; he contrived to "indicate its contiguity, in its most ethereal intangibility, to something that is very plain and deeply practical"; and Pauline Mesh triumphantly embodied it.

Howells stated that "the vehicle" was "delicious" and that the study pleased him throughout. He remarked in particular, however, about his satisfaction with the maiden aunt's rage when her nephew had blown her "a five-fingered kiss" and with the description of the horse-car. He had been delighted with the mother's "struggles—herculean struggles—with such shadowy problems" and with the son who had "the sincere Europeanism of an inalienable, wholly uninspired American."

In 1884 James wrote to Howells from Paris:

> ". . . . The floods of tepid soap and water which under the name of novels are being vomited forth in England, seem to me, by contrast [to Daudet, Goncourt and Zola] to do little honour for our race. I say this to you, because I regard you as the great American naturalist. I don't think you go far enough, and you are haunted with romantic phantoms and a tendency to factitious glosses; but you are in the right path, and I wish you repeated triumphs there. . . . It isn't for me to reproach you . . . the said gloss being a constant defect of *my* characters; they have too much of it—too damnably much. But I am a failure!—comparatively. Read Zola's last thing: *La Joie de Vivre*. The title of course has a desparate irony: but the work is admirably solid and serious. . . . It is rather hard that as you are the only English novelist I read (except Miss Woolson), I should not have more comfort with you."[3]

When James wrote in 1886 his essay about Howells' publications for *Harper's Weekly,* he remarked about his fame abroad because of the increase of interest in the United States, his "copiousness without detriment to his freshness," his constantly enlarged scope, and his "definite and downright convictions" about realism as opposed to romanticism which were the "source of much of the interest that he excites." After discussing Howells' insistence upon recognition in fiction of the "common, the immediate, the familiar and vulgar elements of life," James remarked that Howells looked "askance at exceptions and perversities and superiorities, at surprising and incongruous phenomena in general." James then insisted, however, that "the world is very large, and life is a mixture of many things; she by no means eschews the strange, and often risks combinations and effects that make one rub one's eyes. Nevertheless, Mr. Howells' standpoint is an excellent one for seeing a large part of the truth, and even if it were less advantageous, there would be a great deal to admire in the firmness with which he has planted himself."

James then remarked about Howells' portrayal of American life and of women—and without doubt he had in mind the difficulties his *Daisy Miller* and his *Hawthorne* had caused him:

> "The picture of American life on Mr. Howells' canvas is not of a dazzling brightness, and my readers have probably wondered why it is that (among sensitive people) he has so successfully escaped the imputation of a want of patriotism. The manners he describes—the desolation of the whole social prospect in *A Modern Instance* is perhaps the strongest expression of those influences—are eminently of a nature to discourage the intending visitor, and yet the westward pilgrim continues to arrive, in spite of Bartley Hubbards and Laphams, and the terrible practices at the country hotel in *Doctor Breen,* and at the Boston

boarding-house in *A Woman's Reason.* This tolerance of depressing revelations is explained partly, no doubt, by the fact that Mr. Howells' truthfulness imposes itself—the representation is so vivid that the reader accepts it as he accepts, in his own affairs, the mystery of fate—and partly by a very different consideration, which is simply that if many of his characters are disagreeable, almost all of them are extraordinarily good, and with a goodness which is a ground for national complacency. If American life is on the whole, as I make no doubt whatever, more innocent than that of any other country, nowhere is the fact more patent than in Mr. Howells' novels, which exhibit so constant a study of the actual and so small a perception of evil. His women, in particular, are of the best—except, indeed, in the sense of being the best to live with. Purity of life, fineness of conscience, benevolence of motive, decency of speech, good nature, kindless, charity, tolerance (though, indeed, there is little but each other's manners for the people to tolerate), govern all the scene; the only immoralities are aberrations of thought, like that of Silas Lapham, or excesses of beer, like that of Bartley Hubbard. In the gallery of Mr. Howells' portraits there are none more living than the admirable, humorous images of those two ineffectual sinners. Lapham, in particular, is magnificent, understood down to the ground, inside and out—a creation which does Mr. Howells the highest honor. . . .

After his comments about the lack of perception of evil in the works of Howells, James also characteristically took him to task for his attitude toward style:

". . . . . I should like . . . to allude in passing, for purposes of respectful remonstrance, to a phrase that he suffered the other day to fall from his pen (in a periodical, but not in a novel), to the effect that the style of a work of fiction is a thing that matters less and less all the while.

> Why less and less? It seems to me as great a mistake to say so as it would be to say that it matters more and more. It is difficult to see how it can matter either less or more. The style of a novel is a part of the execution of a work of art; the execution of a work of art is a part of its very essense, and that, it seems to me, must have mattered in all ages exactly the same degree, and be destined always to do so. I can conceive of no state of civilization in which it shall not be deemed important, though of course there are states in which executants are clumsy. I should also venture to express a certain regret that Mr. Howells (whose style, in practice, after all, as I have intimated, treats itself to felicities which his theory perhaps would comdemn) should appear increasingly to hold composition too cheap—by which I mean, should neglect the effect that comes from alternation, distribution, relief. He has an increasing tendency to tell his story altogether in conversations, so that a critical reader sometimes wishes, not that the dialogue might be suppressed (it is too good for that), but that it might be distributed, interspaced with narrative and pictorial matter."

After resigning from the *Atlantic,* Howells contributed articles to it and to *Harper's Monthly* and to *Century Magazine.* In January, 1886, he began writing for *Harper's* the monthly essay called "The Editor's Study" which he contributed until March, 1892. On December 25, 1886, Howells remarked to James in a letter that he "now read a good deal for reviewing, or whatever my work in *Harper's* may be called." He had not read James's latest works—*The Bostonians* and *Princess Casimassima*—for he was leaving them unread until he had "occasion to talk of them." He stated, however, that he knew certain passages and characters in *The Bostonians* quite well and that he thought Olive Chancellor "miraculously good." He knew nothing about the *Princess Casimassima,* but he had heard Lowell proclaiming it to be James's best book and had heard "only good talk of it on all hands." Later in the letter, Howells stated that he had read James's *Little Tour in France,* had found it "delightful reading," and had remarked in it "a more absolute transference to literature of the mood of observation than anything else" he knew.

After remarking that he had been told that *Harper's* had been pleased with the new story received from James, Howells stated that he was glad—rejoiced, in fact—that the story was "on international ground." He had told the editorial staff of *Harper's* that he hoped James would never permit himself "to be disturbed by any outside influence" and then he stressed to James that this area or subject was "pre-eminently and indefeasibly" his territory and that he had "made it, as if it were a bit of the Back Bay." To Howells the possibilities of development of the international story seemed endless for he remarked that "the character that must pass under your eye is increasingly vast in quantity."

Although Howells never reviewed *The Bostonians,* he did review *The Princess Casimassima* in April, 1887, for *Harper's.* Howells' review—included in this collection—was enthusiastic; and one reason the novel was "great," or James's "greatest" one, may have been because it, as Howells remarked, "has to do with socialism and the question of richer and poorer, which grows ever more burning in our day. . . ." Howells was at this time bravely trying to win a stay of execution for the men supposedly involved in the Chicago Haymarket Riot of 1886; he had risked his position and reputation by publishing a letter in defense of the condemned men in the New York *Tribune.* In 1886 Howells had been changed by the reading of Tolstoy; and in 1888 he was to be further influenced by reading Edward Bellamy's *Looking Backward* and by the Nationalist movement which it prompted.[4] Howells was traveling down the road toward Christian socialism which was to alter the substance of his fiction and which was to separate him ideologically from his good friend James.

Although Lowell and Howells considered *The Princess Casimassima* one of James's best and although *The Bostonians* shocked many of the literati, both novels were failures. Since James had aspired to win fame, or at least, an audience with these two publications, he was greatly depressed. Disappointed though he was, James began at this period one of his most ambitious books: *The Tragic Muse*. In January, 1888, he wrote to Howells:

> "I have entered upon evil days. . . . I am still staggering a good deal under the mysterious and (to me) inexplicable injury wrought—apparently—upon my situation by my last two novels . . . from which I expected so much and derived so little. They have reduced the desire and the demand, for my production to zero."[5]

On April 15, 1888, Howells wrote an interesting albeit critical comment about James to Thomas S. Perry: "You'll see James's extraordinary *tour de force* about Stevenson in the *Century* for April. It is really the most remarkable piece of shinning around the question I ever saw. I fancy it was something he was asked to do." Howells without doubt made this disparaging remark about James's article because of his own ill-feeling about Stevenson. In December, 1882, Stevenson had been eager to meet Howells, but, when he read *A Modern Instance* and mistakenly deemed it to be opposed to divorce, he wrote Howells an insulting letter informing him that he could not be his guest because he desired "to know no one who considers himself holier" than Mrs. Stevenson—a divorcee. Howells did not reply to Stevenson's letter, and eventually friendly relationships were restored between the two writers.

In October, 1888, Howells wrote a review of five of James's

stories which had appeared almost simultaneously in four major periodicals: "The Aspern Papers," "The Liar," "A London Life," "Louisa Pallant," and "Two Countries." In this review, included in this collection, Howells extolled the virtues of James which made him a favorite, if not with the critics, with the editors who were "the real avenues to the public." In the same month Howells also published comments about *The Reverberator* in a review which also included Cable's *Bonaventure* and Valdés *The Fourth Estate.*

James must have written Howells a letter expressing his appreciation of Howells' published comments, for on October 10th Howells thanked James for telling him that he had given him pleasure. He stated that he had said what needed to be said and that he only wished that he "could have said them more at length." He then told James that his *Partial Portraits* was "wonderfully good work" and that its contents made his own "critical work seem clumsy and uncouth." With characteristic humility, so far as their friendship was concerned, Howells then commented that James seemed "born with the right word" in his mouth—at least, he never said "the wrong one." He then asserted that there was "distinctly a tendency to a better sense" of James in the United States—if he really cared for "the fat."

Because of Howells' praise in this letter of *Partial Portraits,* it is interesting to recall the commendation which he had made to Perry of the article about Stevenson; for it was included in the collection. Furthermore, it is also notable that James himself did not think that he "was born with the right word" in his mouth, for he constantly revised his novels and short stories before they appeared in book form and even more drastically before they appeared in the New York Edition.

On April 26, 1889, Howells wrote James's sister Alice that her brother had written him a letter about the death of Winifred, his eldest daughter, and that James had expressed himself in perfect terms. Mildred Howells quoted the following excerpt from Howells's letter of March 30th to John Hay: "James wrote to me 'To be young and gentle, and do no harm, and pay for it as if it were a crime.' That is the whole history of our dear girl's life."

Saddened and changed by the death of his daughter, Howells perhaps found solace in writing his *Harper* monthly articles. In any case, he wrote for the August, 1889, issue his review of James's volume of four stories entitled *A London Life*—the last review he was to write about James until he assessed *The Tragic Muse.*

NOTES

[1] Matthiessen reprinted much of this review in *The James Family,* pp. 504-506.

[2] All letters from Howells referred to in this section were printed in full by Mildred Howells, ed., *Life and Letters of William Dean Howels* (1928).

[3] Quoted in Matthiessen, *The James Family,* p. 503.

[4] For a brief review of the literary and political relationships of Howells and Bellamy, see S. E. Bowman, *The Year 2000: A Critical Biography of Edward Bellamy* (1958) and also Joseph Schiffman, "Mutual Indebtedness: Unpublished Letters of Edward Bellamy to William Dean Howells," *Harvard University Bulletin,* X, 3 (Autumn, 1958), pp. 363-374.

[5] Dupee, *Henry James,* p. 140.

HENRY JAMES, JR.*

The events of Mr. James's life—as we agree to understand events—may be told in a very few words. His race is Irish on his father's side and Scotch on his mother's, to which mingled strains the generalizer may attribute, if he likes, that union of vivid expression and dispassionate analysis which has characterized his work from the first. There are none of those early struggles with poverty, which render the lives of so many distinguished Americans monotonous reading, to record in his case: the cabin hearth-fire did not light him to the youthful pursuit of literature; he had from the start all those advantages which, when they go too far, become limitations.

He was born in New York city in the year 1843, and his first lessons in life and letters were the best which the metropolis—so small in the perspective diminishing to that date—could afford. In his twelfth year his family went abroad, and after some stay in England made a long sojourn in France and Switzerland. They returned to America in 1860, placing themselves at Newport, and for a year or two Mr. James was at the Harvard Law School, where, perhaps, he did not study a great deal of law. His father removed from Newport to Cambridge in 1866, and there Mr. James remained till he went abroad, three years later, for the residence in England and Italy which, with infrequent visits home, has continued ever since.

It was during these three years of his Cambridge life that I

* *The Century Magazine* (November, 1882).

became acquainted with his work. He had already printed a tale—"The Story of a Year"—in the "Atlantic Monthly," when I was asked to be Mr. Fields's assistant in the management, and it was my fortune to read Mr. James's second contribution in manuscript. "Would you take it?" asked my chief. "Yes, and all the stories you can get from the writer." One is much securer of one's judgment at twenty-nine than, say, at forty-five; but if this was a mistake of mine I am not yet old enough to regret it. The story was called "Poor Richard," and it dealt with the conscience of a man very much in love with a woman who loved his rival. He told this rival a lie, which sent him away to his death on the field,—in that day nearly every fictitious personage had something to do with the war,—but Poor Richard's lie did not win him his love. It still seems to me that the situation was strongly and finely felt. One's pity went, as it should, with the liar; but the whole story had a pathos which lingers in my mind equally with a sense of the new literary qualities which gave me such delight in it. I admired, as we must in all that Mr. James has written, the finished workmanship in which there is no loss of vigor; the luminous and uncommon use of words, the originality of phrase, the whole clear and beautiful style, which I confess I weakly liked the better for the occasional gallicisms remaining from an inveterate habit of French. Those who know the writings of Mr. Henry James will recognize the inherited felicity of diction which is so striking in the writings of Mr. Henry James, Jr. The son's diction is not so racy as the father's; it lacks its daring, but it is as fortunate and graphic; and I cannot give it greater praise than this, though it has, when he will, a splendor and state which is wholly its own.

Mr. James is now so universally recognized that I shall seem to be making an unwarrantable claim when I express my belief that the popularity of his stories was once largely confined to Mr. Fields's assistant. They had characteristics which forbade any editor to refuse them; and there are no anecdotes of thrice-rejected manuscripts finally printed to tell of him; his work was at once successful with all the magazines. But with the readers of "The Atlantic," of "Harper's," of "Lippincott's," of "The Galaxy," of "The Century," it was another affair. The flavor was so strange, that, with rare exceptions, they had to "learn to like" it. Probably few writers have in the same degree compelled the liking of their readers. He was reluctantly accepted, partly through a mistake as to his attitude—through the confusion of his point of view with his private opinion—in the reader's mind. This confusion caused the tears of rage which bedewed our continent in behalf of the "average American girl" supposed to be satirized in Daisy Miller, and prevented the perception of the fact that, so far as the average American girl was studied at all in Daisy Miller, her indestructible innocence, her invulnerable new-worldliness, had never been so delicately appreciated. It was so plain that Mr. James disliked her vulgar conditions, that the very people to whom he revealed her essential sweetness and light were furious that he should have seemed not to see what existed through him. In other words, they would have liked him better if he had been a worse artist—if he had been a little more confidential.

But that artistic impartiality which puzzled so many in the treatment of Daisy Miller is one of the qualities most valuable in the eyes of those who care how things are done, and I am not sure that it is not Mr. James's most characteristic quality. As "frost performs the effect of fire," this impartiality comes at last to the same result as sympathy. We may be quite sure that Mr. James does not like the peculiar phase of our civilization typified in Henrietta Stackpole; but he treats her with such exquisite justice that he lets *us* like her. It is an extreme case, but I confidently allege it in proof.

His impartiality is part of the reserve with which he works

in most respects, and which at first glance makes us say that he is wanting in humor. But I feel pretty certain that Mr. James has not been able to disinherit himself to this degree. We Americans are terribly in earnest about making ourselves, individually and collectively; but I fancy that our prevailing mood in the face of all problems is that of an abiding faith which can afford to be funny. He has himself indicated that we have, as a nation, as a people, our joke, and every one of us is in the joke more or less. We may, some of us, dislike it extremely, disapprove it wholly, and even abhor it, but we are in the joke all the same, and no one of us is safe from becoming the great American humorist at any given moment. The danger is not apparent in Mr. James's case, and I confess that I read him with a relief in the comparative immunity that he affords from the national facetiousness. Many of his people are humorously imagined, or rather humorously *seen*, like Daisy Miller's mother, but these do not give a dominant color; the business in hand is commonly serious, and the droll people are subordinated. They abound, nevertheless, and many of them are perfectly new finds, like Mr. Tristram in "The American," the bill-paying father in the "Pension Beaurepas," the anxiously Europeanizing mother in the same story, the amusing little Madame de Belgarde, Henrietta Stackpole, and even Newman himself. But though Mr. James portrays the humorous in character, he is decidedly not on humorous terms with his reader; he ignores rather than recognizes the fact that they are both in the joke.

If we take him at all we must take him on his own ground, for clearly he will not come to ours. We must make concessions to him, not in this respect only, but in several others, chief among which is the motive for reading fiction. By example, at least, he teaches that it is the pursuit and not the end which should give us pleasure; for he often prefers to leave us to our own conjectures in regard to the fate of the people in whom he has interested us. There is no question, of course, but he could tell the story of Isabel in "The Portrait of a Lady" to the end, yet he does not tell it. We must agree, then, to take what seems a fragment instead of a whole, and to find, when we can, a name for this new kind in fiction. Evidently it is the character, not the fate, of his people which occupies him; when he has fully developed their character he leaves them to what destiny the reader pleases.

The analytic tendency seems to have increased with him as his work has gone on. Some of the earlier tales were very dramatic: "A Passionate Pilgrim," which I should rank above all his other short stories, and for certain rich poetical qualities, above everything else that he has done, is eminently dramatic. But I do not find much that I should call dramatic in "The Portrait of a Lady," while I do find in it an amount of analysis which I should call superabundance if it were not all such good literature. The novelist's main business is to possess his reader with a due conception of his characters and the situations in which they find themselves. If he does more or less than this he equally fails. I have sometimes thought that Mr. James's danger was to do more, but when I have been ready to declare this excess an error of his method I have hestitated. Could anything be superfluous that had given me so much pleasure as I read? Certainly from only one point of view, and this a rather narrow, technical one. It seems to me that an enlightened criticism will recognize in Mr. James's fiction a metaphysical genius working to aesthetic results, and will not be disposed to deny it any method it chooses to employ. No other novelist, except George Eliot, has dealt so largely in analysis of motive, has so fully explained and commented upon the springs of action in the persons of the drama, both before and after the facts. These novelists are more alike than any others in their processes, but with George Eliot an ethical purpose is dominant, and with Mr. James an artistic purpose. I do not know just how it should be stated of two such noble and generous types of character as Dorothea and Isabel Archer, but I think that we sympathize with the former in grand aims that chiefly concern others, and with the latter in beautiful dreams that primarily concern herself. Both are unselfish and devoted women, sublimely true to a mistaken ideal in their marriages; but, though they come to this common martyrdom, the original difference in them remains. Isabel has her great weaknesses, as Dorothea had, but these seem to me, on the whole, the most nobly intentioned women in modern fiction; and I think Isabel is the more subtly divined of the two. If we speak of mere characterization, we must not fail to acknowledge the perfection of Gilbert Osmond. It was a profound stroke to make him an American by birth. No European could realize so fully in his own life the ideal of a European *dilettante* in all the meaning of that cheapened word; as no European could so deeply and tenderly feel the sweetness and loveliness of the English past as the sick American, Searle, in "The Passionate Pilgrim."

What is called the international novel is popularly dated from the publication of "Daisy Miller," though "Roderick Hudson" and "The American" had gone before; but it really began in the beautiful story which I have just named. Mr. James, who invented this species in fiction, first contrasted in the "Passionate Pilgrim" the New World and Old World moods, ideals, and prejudices, and he did it there with a richness of poetic effect which he has since never equalled. I own that I regret the loss of the poetry, but you cannot ask a man to keep on being a poet for you; it is hardly for him to choose; yet I compare rather discontentedly in my own mind such impassioned creations as Searle and the painter in "The Madonna of the Future" with "Daisy Miller," of whose slight, thin personality I also feel the indefinable charm, and of the tragedy of whose innocence I recognize the delicate pathos. Looking back to those early stories, where Mr. James stood at the dividing ways of the novel and the romance, I am sometimes sorry that he declared even superficially for the former. His best efforts seem to me those of romance; his best types have an ideal development, like Isabel and Claire Belgarde and Bessy Alden and poor Daisy and even Newman. But, doubtless, he has chosen wisely; perhaps the romance is an outworn form, and would not lend itself to the reproduction of even the ideality of modern life. I myself waver somewhat in my preference—if it is a preference—when I think of such people as Lord Warburton and the Touchetts, whom I take to be all decidedly of this world. The first of these especially interested me as a probable type of the English nobleman, who amiably accepts the existing situation with all its possibilities of political and social change, and insists not at all upon the surviving feudalities, but means to be a manly and simple gentleman in any event. An American is not able to pronounce as to the verity of the type; I only know that it seems probable and that it is charming. It makes one wish that it were in Mr. James's way to paint in some story the present phase of change in England. A titled personage is still mainly an inconceivable being to us; he is like a goblin or a fairy in a storybook. How does he comport himself in the face of all the changes and modifications that have taken place and that still impend? We can hardly imagine a lord taking his nobility seriously; it is some hint of the conditional frame of Lord Warburton's mind that makes him imaginable and delightful to us.

It is not my purpose here to review any of Mr. James's books; I like better to speak of his people than of the conduct of his novels, and I wish to recognize the fineness with which he has touched-in the pretty primness of Osmond's daughter and the mild devotedness of Mr. Rosier. A masterly hand is as often manifest in the treatment of such subordinate figures as in that of the principal persons, and Mr. James does them unerringly. This is felt in the more important character of Valentin

Belgarde, a fascinating character in spite of its defects,—perhaps on account of them—and a sort of French Lord Warburton, but wittier, and not so good. "These are my ideas," says his sister-in-law, at the end of a number of inanities. "Ah, you call them ideas!" he returns, which is delicious and makes you love him. He, too, has his moments of misgiving, apparently in regard to his nobility, and his acceptance of Newman on the basis of something like "manhood suffrage" is very charming. It is of course difficult for a remote plebeian to verify the pictures of legitimist society in "The American," but there is the probable suggestion in them of conditions and principles, and want of principles, of which we get glimpses in our travels abroad; at any rate, they reveal another and not impossible world, and it is fine to have Newman discover that the opinions and criticisms of our world are so absolutely valueless in that sphere that his knowledge of the infamous crime of the mother and brother of his betrothed will have no effect whatever upon them in their own circle if he explodes it there. This seems like aristocracy indeed! and one admires, almost respects, its survival in our day. But I always regretted that Newman's discovery seemed the precursor of his magnanimous resolution not to avenge himself; it weakened the effect of this, with which it had really nothing to do. Upon the whole, however, Newman is an adequate and satisfying representative of Americanism, with his generous matrimonial ambition, his vast good-nature, and his thorough good sense and right feeling. We must be very hard to please if we are not pleased with him. He is not the "cultivated American" who redeems us from time to time in the eyes of Europe; but he is unquestionably more national, and it is observable that his unaffected fellow-countrymen and women fare very well at Mr. James's hands always; it is the Europeanizing sort like the critical little Bostonian in the "Bundle of Letters," the ladies shocked at Daisy Miller, the mother in the "Pension Beaurepas" who goes about trying to be of the "native" world everywhere, Madame Merle and Gilbert Osmond, Miss Light and her mother, who have reason to complain, if any one has. Doubtless Mr. James does not mean to satirize such Americans, but it is interesting to note how they strike such a keen observer. We are certainly not allowed to like them, and the other sort find somehow a place in our affections along with his good Europeans. It is a little odd, by the way, that in all the printed talk about Mr. James—and there has been no end of it—his power of engaging your preference for certain of his people has been so little commented on. Perhaps it is because he makes no obvious appeal for them; but one likes such men as Lord Warburton, Newman, Valentin, the artistic brother in "The Europeans," and Ralph Touchett, and such women as Isabel, Claire Belgarde, Mrs. Tristram, and certain others, with a thoroughness that is one of the best testimonies to their vitality. This comes about through their own qualities, and is not affected by insinuation or by downright *petting*, such as we find in Dickens nearly always and in Thackeray too often.

The art of fiction has, in fact, become a finer art in our day than it was with Dickens and Thackeray. We could not suffer the confidential attitude of the latter now, nor the mannerism of the former, any more than we could endure the prolixity of Richardson or the coarseness of Fielding. These great men are of the past—they and their methods and interests; even Trollope and Reade are not of the present. The new school derives from Hawthorne and George Eliot rather than any others; but it studies human nature much more in its wonted aspects, and finds its ethical and dramatic examples in the operation of lighter but not really less vital motives. The moving accident is certainly not its trade; and it prefers to avoid all manner of dire catastrophes. It is largely influenced by French fiction in form; but it is the realism of Daudet rather than the realism of Zola that prevails with it, and it has a soul of its own which is above the business of recording the rather brutish pursuit of a woman by a man, which seems to be the chief end of the French novelist. This school, which is so largely of the future as well as the present, finds its chief exemplar in Mr. James; it is he who is shaping and directing American fiction, at least. It is the ambition of the younger contributors to write like him; he has his following more distinctly recognizable than that of any other English-writing novelist. Whether he will so far control this following as to decide the nature of the novel with us remains to be seen. Will the reader be content to accept a novel which is an analytic study rather than a story, which is apt to leave him arbiter of the destiny of the author's creations? Will he find his account in the unflagging interest of their development? Mr. James's growing popularity seems to suggest that this may be the case; but the work of Mr. James's imitators will have much to do with the final result.

In the meantime it is not surprising that he has his imitators. Whatever exceptions we take to his methods or his results, we cannot deny him a very great literary genius. To me there is a perpetual delight in his way of saying things, and I cannot wonder that younger men try to catch the trick of it. The disappointing thing for them is that it is not a trick, but an inherent virtue. His style is, upon the whole, better than that of any other novelist I know; it is always easy, without being trivial, and it is often stately, without being stiff; it gives a charm to everything he writes; and he has written so much and in such various directions, that we should be judging him very incompletely if we considered him only as a novelist. His book of European sketches must rank him with the most enlightened and agreeable travelers; and it might be fitly supplemented from his uncollected papers with a volume of American sketches. In his essays on modern French writers he indicates his critical range and grasp; but he scarcely does more, as his criticisms in "The Atlantic" and "The Nation" and elsewhere could abundantly testify.

There are indeed those who insist that criticism is his true vocation, and are impatient of his devotion to fiction; but I suspect that these admirers are mistaken. A novelist he is not, after the old fashion, or after any fashion but his own; yet since he has finally made his public in his own way of storytelling—or call it character-painting if you prefer,—it must be conceded that he has chosen best for himself and his readers in choosing the form of fiction for what he has to say. It is, after all, what a writer has to say rather than what he has to tell that we care for nowadays. In one manner or other the stories were all told long ago; and now we want merely to know what the novelist thinks about persons and situations. Mr. James gratifies this philosophic desire. If he sometimes forbears to tell us what he thinks of the last state of his people, it is perhaps because that does not interest him, and a large-minded criticism might well insist that it was childish to demand that it must interest him.

I am not sure that my criticism is sufficiently large-minded for this. I own that I like a finished story; but then also I like those which Mr. James seems not to finish. This is probably the position of most of his readers, who cannot very logically account for either preference. We can only make sure that we have here an annalist, or analyst, as we choose, who fascinates us from his first page to his last, whose narrative or whose comment may enter into any minuteness of detail without fatiguing us, and can only truly grieve us when it ceases.

PRINCESS CASAMASSIMA*

We find *no* fault with Mr. Henry James's *Princess Casamassima*: it is a great novel; it is his greatest, and it is incomparably the greatest novel of the year in our language. It has to do with socialism and the question of richer and poorer, which grows ever more burning in our day, and the scene is contemporary London. Its people are the types which the vast range of London life affords, and they are drawn not only from the highest and the lowest, but from the intermediate classes, who are so much more difficult to take alive. The Princess Casamassima is our old acquaintance Miss Light, of *Roderick Hudson* fame, come with her beauty and splendor to forget her hated husband in semi-sincere sympathy with the London socialists, and semi-personal lovemaking with two of the handsomest. The hero is the little, morbid, manly, aesthetic bookbinder Hyacinth Robinson, son of an English lord and a French girl, who kills her betrayer. For the climax, Robinson, remembering his mother, kills himself—inevitably, not exemplarily—rather than shoot the political enemy whom the socialists have devoted to death at his hand. A striking figure is the plain, good, simple, romantic Lady Aurora, who goes about among the poor, and loves the tough-hearted chemist's assistant, Paul Muniment, and devotes herself to his sister, the unconsciously selfish little cripple. Another is Pynsent, the old dress-maker, who has brought Robinson up, and who lives and dies in awe

* *Harper's New Monthly Magazine* (April, 1887).

of him as an offshoot of the aristocracy; another is Captain Sholto, the big, handsome, aimless swell, *dilettante* socialist, and hopeless lover of the Princess; another the Prince, with his passion for his wife and his coarse primitive jealousy of her; others yet are the real socialists—English, French, and German; and the ferment of the ideals and interests of all these is the story. From first to last we find no weakness in the book; the drama works simply and naturally; the causes and effects are logically related; the theme is made literature without ceasing to be life. There is an easy breadth of view and a generous scope which recall the best Russian work; and there is a sympathy for the suffering and aspiration in the book which should be apparent even to the critical groundlings, though Mr. James forbears, as ever, to pat his people on the back, to weep upon their necks, or to caress them with endearing and compassionate epithets and pet names. A mighty good figure, which we had almost failed to speak of, is the great handsome shop-girl Millicent Henning, in whose vulgar good sense and vulgar good heart the troubled soul of Hyacinth Robinson finds what little repose it knows.

Mr. James's knowledge of London is one of the things that strike the reader most vividly, but the management of his knowledge is vastly more important. If any one would see plainly the difference between the novelist's work and the partisan's work, let him compare *The Princess Casamassima* and Mr. W. H. Mallock's last tract, which he calls *The Old Order Changes,* and which also deals with socialism. No one can read it and deny Mr. Mallock's extraordinary cleverness, or its futility. His people are apparently real people till he gets them into his book, and then they turn into stalking-horses for his opinions, those who would naturally disagree with him coming helplessly forward to be overthrown by those wonderful Roman Catholics of his—so very, very fine; so very, very wise; so very, very rich; so very, very good; so very, very proud and wellborn. We have some glimpses of an American girl, who seems at first a reality; but she ends by turning into an impossibility to oblige the author.*

* Howells' brief but excellent review of *The Princess Casamassima* appeared at the end of a long article in the April, 1887, "Editor's Study," *Harper's Monthly*. This article about James's book was controversial, and Howells reprinted a large part of it in *Criticism and Fiction* (Chapter XVII, p. 95). In this reprinted section he stated his objections to what he considered "unmoral" novels: " 'If a novel flatters the passions, and exalts them above the principles, it is poisonous . . . so-called unmoral romances, which imagine a world where the sins of the senses are unvisited by the penalties following, swift or slow, but inexorably sure, in the real world, are deadly poison: they do kill.' "

This article irritated Lafcadio Hearn, who devoted an editorial to it in New Orleans *Times-Democrat* of April 12 (reprinted in *Essays on American Literature*, edited by Sanki Ichikawa and with an introduction by Albert Mordell). In this article entitled "One of Howells's Realisms," Hearn said that Howells' dogmas about love and duty as motives in writing novels suggested that the spirit of Howells' inspiration was neo-Puritanism. Hearn maintained that these very senses, sentiments, and perceptions which Howells ignored really moved the world and that Howells was an anomaly for his views indicated either an atrophy or an absence of certain artistic faculties.

Hearn also resented a statement purportedly made by Howells that Miss Murfee ("Charles Egbert Craddock") should not let her fancy begin to work on her mountain folk. Hearn stated that to the mind of the true artist the usual impression and the artistic suggestions of that impression come simultaneously.

In the two other articles which Hearn wrote about Howells, he said in 1886 that Howells suppressed emotion, enthusiasm, and natural feeling in his novels. One year later Hearn nevertheless called Howells a "great novelist."

STORIES REPRINTED IN *THE ASPERN PAPERS* AND *A LONDON LIFE**

It seems to us that the touch of Mr. Henry James is of such excellent maturity in the short stories which he has lately printed that it would be futile to dispute his primacy in most literary respects. We mean his primacy not only among fabling Americans, but among all who are presently writing fiction. It is with an art richly and normally perfected from intentions evident in his earliest work that he now imparts to the reader his own fine sense of character and motive, and gives his conceptions a distinctness and definition really unapproached. There never was much 'prentice faltering in him; the danger was rather that in one so secure of his literary method from the first, a mere literary method might content to the end; but with a widening if not a deepening hold on life (all must admit that his hold has widened, whoever denies that it has deepened) this has clearly not contented him. No one has had more to say to his generation of certain typical phases than he, and he has had incomparably the best manner of saying it. Of course it can always be urged by certain mislikers of his—and he has them in force enough to witness the vast impression he has made—that these typical phases are not the important phases; but if they do this they must choose

* *Harper's New Monthly Magazine* (October, 1888).

["The Aspern Papers", "Louisa Pallant", and "Two Countries" were reprinted in *The Aspern Papers* (1888). "A London Life" and "The Liar" were reprinted in *A London Life* (1889).]

wholly to ignore such a novel as *The Princess Casamassima.* It is in a way discreditable to our time that a writer of such quality should ever have grudging welcome; the fact impeaches not only our intelligence, but our sense of the artistic. It will certainly amaze a future day that such things as his could be done in ours and meet only a feeble and conditional acceptance from the "best" criticism, with something little short of ribald insult from the common cry of literary paragraphers. But happily the critics do not form an author's only readers; they are not even his judges. These are the editors of the magazines, which are now the real avenues to the public; and their recent unanimity in presenting simultaneously some of the best work of Mr. James's life in the way of short stories indicates the existence of an interest in all he does, which is doubtless the true measure of his popularity. With "The Aspern Papers" in *The Atlantic,* "The Liar" in *The Century,* "A London Life" in *Scribner's,* and "Louisa Pallant" and "Two Countries" in *Harper's,* pretty much all at once, the effect was like an artist's exhibition. One turned from one masterpiece to another, making his comparisons, and delighted to find that the stories helped rather than hurt one another, and that their accidental massing enhanced his pleasure in them.

Masterpieces, we say, since the language does not hold their betters for a high perfection of literary execution at all points. "Louisa Pallant," for instance, is an unmixed pleasure if you delight in a well-taken point of view, and then a story that runs easily from the lips of the imagined narrator, characterizing him no less subtly than the persons of the tale, in English to the last degree informal and to the last degree refined. Just for attitude, just for light, firm touch, the piece is simply unsurpassed outside the same author's work. We speak now only of the literature, and leave the doubter to his struggle with the question whether a mother would have done all that about a daughter; and we will not attempt to decide whether the American wife in the "Two Countries" would have killed herself if her English husband had written a book against her native land. These were to us very minor points compared with the truthfulness of the supposed case and the supposed people, just as in "A London Life" it doesn't so much matter whether poor Laura marries or not as whether the portrait of Mr. Wendover is not almost too good to be felt by the public which reads in running, and whether some touch of Selina's precious badness may not be lost. There are depths under depths in the subtle penetrations of this story, the surprise of which should not be suffered to cheapen the more superficial but not less brilliant performance in "The Liar"; for there too is astonishing divination, and a clutch upon the unconscious motives which are scarcely more than impulses, instincts.

James's
THE REVERBERATOR

George W. Cable's
BONAVENTURE

A. P. Valdés'
THE FOURTH ESTATE*

To Mr. Cable in his inter-related sketches called *Bonaventure* we owe the pleasure of some fresh characters in a romantic atmosphere where we could not have hoped for anything better than types. The book is no such book as *The Grandissimes*; let that be fairly understood before we praise it for qualities proper to its slighter texture. *The Grandissimes* is one of the great novels of our time, whereas *Bonaventure* is simply one of the gracefulest romances, in which high motive, generous purpose, and picturesque material answer for the powerful realities of the other. The facts of the case—the aspiration and the heroic self-sacrifice of the young creole school-master among the Acadians of Louisiana—are given by a species of indirection, a kind of tacking, which recalls Judd's method in his *Margaret*, a book which Mr. Cable could not have had in mind, but to which his work assimilates itself in the romantic atmosphere common to them both. It has its charm, but it also has a misty intangibility which baffles, which vexes. Never-

* *Harper's New Monthly Magazine* (October, 1888).

theless this too is the work of a master who gives us for the time what he thinks best, and who has not yet begun to deliver his whole message to a world where few of the prophets have both head and heart. We see in him a curious process of evolution, in which the citizen, the Christian, seems to threaten the artist; but out of which we trust to see them issue in indissoluble alliance for the performance of services to humanity higher than any yet attempted. It is the conscience of Mr. Cable that gives final value to all he does; it will avail him with readers similarly endowed against any provincial censure, and will not suffer him to slight any side of his most important work, or to forget that art is the clearest medium of truth.

It is a very delicate medium, however, and it breaks unless the ethical intention it is meant to carry is very carefully adjusted.

It was not because the censure of Mr. Cable was sectional or local that we were tempted just now to call it provincial, but because it was narrow-minded, the censure of people who would rather be flattered than appreciated; and in this sort the sum of our national censure of Mr. James is provincial. It is extraordinary that any one could read *The Reverberator* and not cry out in grateful recognition of its thorough Americanism; it makes one afraid that the author's patriotism has mistaken us, and that we are really a nation of snobs, who would rather be supposed to have fine manners than good qualities; or that we are stupid, and cannot perceive the delicate justice that rights us in spite of ourselves. But there is no mistake in his art, which, beginning with such a group of Americans as the Dossons and their friend the reporter of the society newspaper on the plane of their superficial vulgarity, ends with having touched into notice every generous and valuable point in them, and espoused their cause against that of the grander world. In the case of the obtuse Flack this effect is almost miraculous, in that of Mr. Dosson and his daughter Delia it is charming, and in that of Francie Dosson adorable. We leave the Probert group of Gallicized Americans to those who know them better, though Francie's lover Gaston goes to one's heart; but the Dossons are all true and verifiable in their inexpugnable innocence at any turn in the international world which Mr. James has discovered for us. Francie Dosson, with her beauty, her fineness, her goodness, and her helpless truth, is a marvellous expression of the best in American girlhood. She unwittingly does her lover's people an awful mischief, and to the end she remains half persuaded of Mr. Flack's theory that people really like to have their private affairs written up in the papers; but all the same she remains lovable, and Gaston loves her. "*Sie war liebenswürdig und er liebte sie.*" Mr. James makes you feel once again that this settles it.

As for Flack, he is perfect, the very genius of society journalism. But apparently, however indigenous with us, his species is not confined to our own country in its origin, if we may believe Señor Valdés in his latest novel, *El Cuarto Poder*, or *The Fourth Estate*, or the newspaper press mainly as it exists in the little seaport city of Sarrió, somewhere in northwestern Spain of to-day. Sinforoso Suarez is the resonant Spanish of the nature if not of the name of Flack, though with a mellifluousness and a malignity added which are foreign to Flack; for as a rule the American interviewer wishes his victim no harm, and does not ordinarily aim at fine writing even when he achieves it. But, as in Mr. James's story, journalism is a subordinate interest of Señor Valdés's novel, which is mainly a picture of contemporary life in a Spanish town. The reader of these pages need be at no loss to conjecture our opinion of this author's work, and from the versions of his *Marquis of Peñalta* and his *Maximina* any English reader can test it for himself. We will only say that, without their unity, *El Cuarto Poder* is in other respects a greater work than either; its range is vaster, its tolerance as charming, its sympathy with all good things as pervasive, its humor delicious. Don Rosendo Bellinchón and the cigar girl whom he marries; their son Pablo, from boyhood to youth immoral, reckless, and cowardly; and their daughters Cecilia and Ventura, are, with Gonzalo de las Cuevas, the husband of Ventura, the principal persons, around whom are grouped the vividly painted *personnel* and circumstance of Sarrió. The novel is mainly the tragic story of Gonzalo, who abandons Cecilia and marries Ventura, and experiences through her ambition and treachery the truth of his uncle's saying, that God himself cannot help the man who breaks his word. But he is not a false person, only simply, helplessly true, and there grows up between him and Cecilia the sweetest and purest friendship ever imagined in fiction: it is most beautifully and courageously done; it consoles him in the worst affliction, but it cannot save him. Spanish aristocracy as it survives, intellectualized and agnosticized, into modern times is studied with irony that would be bitter, if Valdés could be bitter, in the Duque de Tornos, who seduces the ready Ventura; and a whole population of middle-class and plebeian figures live in the author's humorous sympathy.

Bellinchón himself is a character worthy of Cervantes, with his extravagancies and contradictions, and his wife, with her growth through sorrow into a refinement not otherwise possible to her simple goodness, is a lovely creation. It is impossible to touch the merit of the book at all points; it has in one romantic excess of self-sacrifice a single important fault; but it has that frankness, of which we must advise the intending reader, characteristic of Latin writers in treating Latin life; that is to say, Sarrió is not described as if it were Salem, Massachusetts.

A LONDON LIFE *

We have spoken already of *A London Life,* which while it was still a serial seemed to us so extraordinarily good in prospect. In retrospect it is even better (in the volume of stories which it names); and we invite the reader to notice the sharp severity of moral outline in the American personages against the London background. Good and bad alike, they have carried with them into foreign atmosphere the unsparing definition which all objects wear in ours; when they are not grotesquely intense they are pathetically intense in the strange environment. It is an effect which we notice in one another abroad, and which makes us wonder where in the world all the odd Americans in Europe come from. But we suspect that it is the very accuracy with which Mr. James reproduces it that makes some of us so angry with him for what we call his caricatures of his countrymen, and especially his country-women. They are really not caricatures: a caricature of any sort would be impossible to his delicate art: they are exact portraits, and not the less perfectly realized because they seem so pitiless. One cannot accuse him of drawing the English people in *The Liar* with unnatural tenderness; yet the worst of them has a softer psychological outline than that charming, that thoroughly good American girl, Laura Wing, in *A London Life,* whose most tremulous uncertainties are all so distinct. That group of varied Bostonians on *The Patagonia* is something to make one

* *Harper's New Monthly Magazine* (August, 1889).

shiver; each seems thrusting a rectangular elbow into one's ribs from a personality as clear cut as the sculpture of long self-consciousness could make it; yet they are only on the way to Europe, and have, as it were, their Back Bay and their South End still about them. They will not show a keener contour against the vague English light when they arrive; it will do its best to mellow their edges; but it will not succeed; and because they will block themselves out in it as sharply as they would against their native sky, they will seem the caricatures which they really are not.

No one but a fine artist like Mr. James would have felt their peculiarity, or had the courage to recognize it in his work; but he must pay the penalty of being true, which attends that sort of conduct pretty unfailingly. He could make himself much more acceptable to his generation if he would treat his negatives a little, and flatter away those hard edges in the process which we believe the photographers call vignetting. But since there is small hope of his making this patriotic sacrifice, we will take what comfort we can from the thought that there must be a compensating advantage spiritually in the definiteness which makes us appear odd socially, even in our own eyes, when we see our pictures.

PART THREE

Howells on the Later Writing of James

1890-1903

INTRODUCTION

From 1890 to 1899, Howells published fifteen volumes; and outstanding among these were three novels which continued the realistic social criticism of *Annie Kilburn*: *A Hazard of New Fortunes* (1890), *The Quality of Mercy* (1892), and *The World of Chance* (1893). The most important novel of this group was *A Hazard of New Fortunes*; and, when James had read it, he wrote on May 16, 1890, to his brother William:

> "I have just been reading with wonder and admiration, Howells's last big novel, which I think is so prodigiously good and able and so beyond what he at one time seemed in danger of reducing himself to, that I mean to write him a gushing letter about it not a day later than tomorrow. . . . His abundance and facility are my constant wonder and envy—or rather not perhaps, envy, inasmuch as he has purchased them by throwing the whole question of form, style and composition overboard into the deep sea—from which, on my side, I am perpetually trying to fish them up."[1]

As he had said he would, James wrote to Howells the following day, May 17, 1890, from Milan:

> "I have not been writing to you at a tremendous, an infamous rate, for a long time past; but I should indeed be sunk in baseness if I were to keep this pace after what has just happened. For what has just happened is that I have

been reading the *Hazard of New Fortunes* (I confess I should have liked to change the name for you,) and that it has filled me with communicable rapture. . . . To my charmed and gratified sense, the *Hazard* is simply prodigious. . . . I should think it would make you as happy as poor happiness will let us be, to turn off from one year to the other, and from a reservoir in daily domestic use, such a free, full, rich flood. In fact your reservoir deluges me, altogether, with surprise as well as other sorts of effusion; by which I mean that though you do much to empty it you keep it remarkably full. I seem myself in comparison to fill mine with a teaspoon and obtain but a trickle. However, I don't mean to compare myself with you or to compare you, in the particular case, with anything but life. When I do that—with the life you see and represent—your faculty for representing it seems to me extraordinary and to shave the truth—the general truth you aim at—several degrees closer than anyone else begins to. You are less *big* than Zola, but are ever so much less clumsy and more really various, and moreover you and he don't see the same things—you have a wholly different consciousness—*you* see a totally different side of a different race. Man isn't at all *one* after all—its take so much of him to be American, to be French, &c. I won't even compare you with something I have a sort of dim stupid sense you might be and are not—for I don't in the least know that you might be it, after all, or whether, if you were, you wouldn't cease to be that something you are which makes me write to you thus. We don't know what people might give us that they don't—the only thing is to take them on what they do and to allow them absolutely and utterly their conditions. This alone, for the tastes, secures freedom of enjoyment. I apply the rule to you, and it represents a perfect triumph of appreciation; because it makes me accept, largely, all your material from you—an absolute gain when I consider that I should never take it from myself. I note certain things which make me wonder

> at your form and your fortune (e.g.—as I have told you before—the fatal colour in which they let *you,* because you live at home—is it?—paint American life; and the fact that there's a whole quarter of heaven upon which, in the matter of composition, you seem consciously—*is* it consciously?—to have turned your back;) but these things have no relevancy whatever as grounds of dislike—simply because you communicate so completely what you undertake to communicate. The novelist is a particular *window,* absolutely—and of worth insofar as he is one; and it's because you open so well and are hung so close over the street that I could hang out of it all day long. Your very value is that you choose your own street—heaven forbid I should have to choose it for you. If I should say I mortally dislike the people who pass in it, I should seem to be taking on myself that intolerable responsibility of selection which is exactly such a luxury to be relieved of. Indeed I'm convinced that no readers above the rank of an idiot—this number is moderate, I admit—really fail to take any view that is really *shown* them—any gift (of subject) that's really given. The usual imbecility of the novel is that the showing and giving simply don't come off—the reader never touches the subject and the subject never touches the reader; the window is no window at all—but only childish *finta,* like the ornaments of our beloved Italy. This is why, as a triumph of *communication,* I hold the *Hazard* so rare and strong. You communicate in touches so close, so fine, so droll so frequent. I am writing too much (you will think me demented with chatter;). . . ."[2]

In August of 1890 William James wrote Howells a glowing letter in which he too asked Howells if he could have written such a "solid piece" ten years before. He commented upon the "intensely individual" but numerous characters, "the everlasting wit and humor," and "beneath all the bass accompaniment of the human problem the entire Americanness of it, all make it a very great book, and one which will last when we shall have melted into the infinite azure." William then added: "The year which shall have witnessed the apparition of your *Hazard of New Fortunes,* Harry's *Tragic Muse,* and of my *Psychology* will indeed be a memorable one in American Literature."[3]

Although *The Tragic Muse* was unfavorably received by most critics, it marked a momentous change in the career of James. First of all, it was the last long novel which employed a somewhat conventional method of narration; second, James was to turn after it to writing dramas, which had long intrigued him, in the hope of winning fame; and third, the short stories —many of them concerned with the problem of the artist— that he wrote after this novel were some of his best.[4] After 1900 he was to produce his most complicated fiction and to write the introductions to the New York Edition which won him everlasting fame and influence in the field of fiction. The famous novels which he produced in his last period were: *The Wings of the Dove* (1902), *The Ambassadors* (1903), and *The Golden Bowl* (1904).

Of the works by James published after 1890, Howells reviewed only *The Tragic Muse, Terminations, The Soft Side,* and *The Letters of Henry James.* He did, however, discuss James's women characters in "Mr. James's *Daisy Miller*; and, in "Mr. Henry James's Later Work," *The Wings of the Dove, The Awkward Age, The Sacred Fount.* In his review of *The Tragic Muse* of September, 1890, which is included in this section, Howells defended James as a modern writer who cared little for a story as such but who used it as a "means," an "end," an illustration. Howells remarked that James's method had always created a "stupid clamor;" and he termed his critics as "nurslings of fable," as ones who had been "pampered to imbecility." To Howells, *The Tragic Muse* "marked the farthest departure from the old ideal of the novel" for no vice was punished, no virtue rewarded. Although he had previously objected to the unfinished endings of James's novels, Howells merely stated that in *The Tragic Muse* "the people are still going uncertainly on as we find people going on in the world about us" and that this "does not prevent our being satisfied with the study of each as we find it in the atelier of a master."

In the same month that Howells published this review, he replied to James's enthusiastic but slightly critical letter about *A Hazard of New Fortunes.* In his letter he commented that *The Tragic Muse* was almost the "tutelary deity of . . . the reading public"—and he hoped that the financial returns from publishers would convince James of the popularity which he reported. Howells remarked that it was unfortunate that James's publishers did not release fifty-cent copies of his novels—as Howells' did—for this method would enable his books to get "into the hands of the people."

Nearly nineteen years later, Howells wrote James about his wife's reaction to *The Tragic Muse* as they read portions of the book aloud every night. Because Mrs. Howells' "nervous strength" was slight and because her interest in the book was so intense, she would seldom permit her husband to read more than twelve pages. She also dreaded finishing the story; for she stated that she did not know where anything else like it could be found—not even if written by James. After remarking that Mrs. Howells no longer cared for many of the occupations she had once enjoyed and after telling how he had asked her just what she did care for, Howells related how touched he had been when his wife had replied that she liked James's "way of doing things—and you." Howells added that he himself was filled with "constantly mounting wonder" at James's " 'way' "—at the "fullness, the closeness, the density of" his work. Once again he depreciated his own fiction by saying that it seemed "so meagre beside" that of his friend.

In his letter to James of February 23, 1892, Howells commented about James's paper about Charles Wolcott Balestier —Kipling's brother-in-law who had collaborated with him in *The Naulahka* (1892). This essay, which was reprinted by Leon Edel in *The American Essays of Henry James,* served as an introduction to *The Average Woman,* a posthumous volume of short stories. To Howells, James's paper about "our dear Balestier" was "absolutely fit"—could not, in fact, have been better. He stated that he would publish it in his first issue of the *Cosmopolitan* (with which he was then briefly associated). He then commented that he had visited in Cambridge and had gone in the "evening to Perry's" where they always talked of James.

During this period in which Howells extolled the virtues of James's literary works, James himself was depressed about his literary career and he expressed from time to time his trepidations in his letters to Howells. On December 13, 1894, Howells wrote his friend about the discouragement James had unjustifiably expressed in his last letter of some weeks before. He told James that his "heart had protested against" his comments "with promptness that" put "his pen to shame;" and he then proceeded to assert that no one in the literary world of the United States had the rank which James held and that it was on James—and not on himself—that the "aspiring eyes are bent of those that hope to do something themselves."

Howells then advised James that, if he would produce a novel of the quality of his "Lesson of the Master" or "The Death of the Lion," he would address a larger audience than he had ever before captured. He was certain that, despite the flood of material being published in the United States by the "little British romanticists," any editor whom James might approach with a story would welcome it. Furthermore, the field of publications was widening—there were to be two new magazines, one in New York and the other in Chicago—and all James had to do was "to come in and occupy it"—and Howells wished he would return home to do so. He wished to talk with him "of all the things which we have in common."

After stating that he was glad that James's "evil dream of the stage" was ended, Howells advised him to devote himself wholly to the novel and not to abandon the international field which he had "created, or at least cleared." Howells remarked that, although James portrayed "English people past all Englishman," no one approached him in depicting "a certain sort of your own countrymen and countrywomen."

Howells cited the reaction of his daughter Mildred who was "*commencement de siècle*" as evidence that James was "very modern." To Mildred, James's Boston types were as true as if they had just been limned. He also stated that his son also appreciated James and that these two young people were representative of a "joy that knows" that was "more largely national" than James, living abroad, could realize. To enforce his statements about the appreciation and opportunities which awaited James, Howells then stated that he had plans for a serial publication in which "three, or four, or five known and 'selected' novelists" would publish their works in "a monthly number." He promised James that he would "appeal" to him to join him if he found a publisher who would accept his scheme.

The consolation Howells' letter was to James may be seen from the reply he wrote to Howells after the disastrous performance of January 5, 1895, in London of his play *Guy Domville,* which, wrote James to William, had been received by "a battle of the most gallant, prolonged, and sustained applause with the hoots and jeers and catcalls of the roughs, whose *roars* . . . were only exacerbated . . . by the conflict. It was a cheering scene, as you may imagine, for a nervous, sensitive, exhausted author to face."[6] In his letter to Howells, James showed that he had sufficiently recovered from his humiliation to make literary plans for the future:

"I am indebted to you for your most benignant letter of December last. It lies open before me and I read it again and am soothed and comforted again. You put your finger sympathetically on the place and spoke of what I wanted you to speak of. I *have* felt, for a long time past, that I have fallen upon evil days—every sign or symbol of one's being in the least *wanted,* anywhere or by any one, having so utterly failed. A new generation, that I know not, and mainly prize not, has taken universal possession. The sense of being utterly out of it weighed me down, and I asked myself what my future would be. All these melancholies were qualified by one redeeming reflection —the sense of how little, for a good while past (for reasons very logical, but accidental and temporary,) I had been producing. I *did* say to myself 'Produce again—produce; produce better than ever, and all will yet be well'; and there was sustenance in that so far as it went. But it has meant much more to me since *you* have said it—for it *is,* practically, what you admirably say. It is exactly, moreover, what I meant to admirably do—and have meant, all along, about this time to get into the motion of. The whole thing, however, represents a great change in my life, inasmuch as what is clear is that periodical publication is practically closed to me—I'm the last hand that the magazines, in this country or in the U. S., seem to want. I won't afflict you with the now accumulated (during all these past years) evidence on which this induction rests —and I have spoken of it to no creature till, at this late day, I speak of it to you. . . . All this, I needn't say, is for your *segretissimo* ear. What it means is that 'production' for me, as aforesaid, means production of the little *book,* pure and simple—independent of any antecedent appearance; and, truth to tell, now that I wholly *see* that, and

> have at last accepted it, I am, incongruously, not at all sorry. I am indeed very serene. I have always hated the magazine form, magazine conditions and manners, and much of the magazine company. I hate the hurried little subordinate part that one plays in the catchpenny picturebook—and the negation of all literature that the insolence of the picturebook imposes. The money-difference will be great—but not so great after a bit as at first; and the other differences will be so all to the good that even from the economic point of view they will tend to make up for that and perhaps finally even completely do so. It is about the distinctness of one's *book-position* that you have so substantially reassured me; and I mean to do far better work than ever I have done before. I have, potentially, improved immensely and am bursting with ideas and subjects—though the act of composition is with me more and more slow, painful and difficult. I shall never again write a long novel; but I hope to write six immortal short ones —and some tales of the same quality. Forgive, my dear Howells, the cynical egotism of these remarks—the fault of which is in your own sympathy."[7]

In his letter James was also preoccupied with the same problems of the writer which he had used as sources for his fiction during the period he had attempted to win fame and fortune as a dramatist. He had dealt with the relationship of the artist, the commercial world, and the public in many of the tales included in *Embarrassments,* as well as in the two stories Howells had mentioned in his letter as examples of what James might write. After his fiasco as a playwright, James solved his own problem as an artist and devoted himself not to winning a public but to "difficulty"—and by this he meant dramatic presentation and discovery of the meaning of life.[8] His success between 1896 and 1901 may be attested to by the listing of the books and novelettes which appeared: *The Other House* (1896), *The Spoils of Poynton* (1897), *The Turn of the Screw*

(1898), *The Awkward Age* (1899), *The Soft Side* (1900), and *The Sacred Fount* (1901).

In 1894 Howells visited his son who was studying in Paris—an event important, as we shall see, to the literary career of James—and he was again in Europe three years later. On December 27, 1897, Howells wrote to Charles Eliot Norton that he had spent two days in London and had seen "James continuously and exclusively." He had, he added, never found James "more divinely interesting"—and he then remarked that James had told him that he had been useful to him, had given him "a new business perspective." James had been "needlessly but deeply discouraged," but Howells had once again been able to "reassure him of his public" in the United States.

Howells also reported to Mark Twain in October, 1898, his reactions to James's dictation of his fiction. He was amused to hear James state that he had begun to dictate all his fiction because he had heard that Howells always did so. Howells remarked that, although James was successful in using this method, he himself could not think of anything that would be worse for him "than a typewriter"—unless "it would be a human typewriter."

On April 17, 1898, Howells reported to James the reactions of his family to the now famous and controversial *Turn of the Screw*, which was then being serialized in *Collier's Weekly*. Howells and his daughter Mildred had—despite James's orders to the contrary—been reading the weekly installments and had "simply jumped up and down between times in . . . impatience." On the other hand, Mrs. Howells had refrained from reading the serial, for she "had been warned by the sight of" her husband's and daughter's sufferings. Howells stated that she was to have her "reward in one gulp"—for the book was being published in *The Two Magics*—but that he and Mildred were "still waiting for the last sip."

Howells stated that he could not imagine how James would end the story and that he really did not care. The important thing was that James had "done it in any event," and he had been so successful that Howells had been more interested in it than in "any ghost story" he had ever read. Although James might think his statement was not significant, he meant, Howells made quite clear, "a lot of praise" for the tale was the kind that he was "fond of."

Turning to the publication of James's "American Letters" in *Literature,* Howells remarked that he had seen the first one published in April but not the second one. Mrs. Howells had so liked the one they had read that she had copied—"for the joy of having it in holograph, apparently"—the passage about the " 'unmitigatible womenkind' " which she thought supreme and which she had already "used effectively in putting" him "to shame for an attempted letter of" his own which he hoped to publish in the same publication. Howells remarked that he hoped James would "read . . . reluctance between the lines" if he saw his article. When it appeared, Howells denounced the war with Spain as stupid and causeless.[9]

On July 31, 1898, Howells wrote James a letter which was occasioned by his having reread James's review of *A Foregone Conclusion,*[10] which had been published in the *North American Review* in 1875. The issue had been loaned by Mrs. Howells to her sister-in-law who had just returned the magazine—nearly twenty-five years later—before the Howells had left New York for York Harbor, Maine. Howells had found the review "something so beautiful and wise that" he was certain James's maturity wouldn't want to disown it." He described his emotional reactions: his "heart warmed itself over in the glow of" James's praise and he had felt himself "thirty-five again, with my years and my novels all before me." After expressing his appreciation for the review, Howells then stated that he had intentions of writing a study of York Harbor for a paper in *Literature*—and he added that he "liked excessively" the material James was publishing in that periodical and that he found his work "excellent in matter and simply bewitching in manner."

On July 15, 1900, Howells wrote about his author-newspaper enterprise which he had hoped to establish and about a James story which was probably to be the tale of terror published posthumously in 1917—*The Sense of the Past.* According to Dupee, Howells had written James in the same year suggesting that he write a "supernatural tale with an American ghost."[11] James began the story of his American who was "magically translated to the England of 1820" and he wrote to Howells about it on June 29th. He then abandoned it and did not return to it until 1914; he was occupied, as we shall see, with writing *The Ambassadors.*

Howells mentioned the possible publication of James's "spectre" in his publishing enterprise, but he also warned him that he did not want him to create his tale of terror without being apprised of the possibility that his venture might fail the spectre "at the very hour when he needs its support." If James could really—as he had stated—easily place the story, Howells then advised him to "go gaily on." He stated also that he himself felt the "chances were so good that they" were "worth trying for" and that, whether or not he continued as editor of the project, he was going to contribute a book.

This letter is of particular interest because it shows the lengths to which Howells was willing to go with his advice and his help. He not only advised James to take "the proffered $2500, rather than the percentage on sales" but offered to do his bargaining for him with "the enterpriser." He made this offer because, as he stated, he believed he could "get better terms than" James could.

James replied to Howells that he now had a new preoccupation, *The Ambassadors*:

"Preoccupied with . . . things of the altogether human order now fermenting in my brain, I don't care for 'terror' (terror, that is, without pity) so much as I otherwise might. . . . The scheme to which I am now alluding is lovely—human, dramatic, international, exquisitely 'pure,' exquisitely everything; only absolutely condemned, from the germ up, to be workable in not less than 100,000 words. If 100,000 words were what you had asked me for, I would fall back upon it ('terror' failing) like a flash, and even send you without a delay, a detailed Scenario of it that I drew up a year ago; beginning then—a year ago—to *do* the thing—immediately afterwards; and then again pausing for reasons extraneous and economic. . . . It really constitutes, at any rate, the work I intimately want actually to be getting on with. . . . My genius, I may even say, absolutely thrives—and I am unbrokenly yours."[12]

After James had completed *The Ambassadors* in 1901 (it was not published until 1903), he told Howells about the germ of the story—a remark Howells had made when he was in Paris in 1894 at Whistler's home. As James recorded the story told him by Jonathan Sturges in his notebook entry of October 31, 1895, Howells, who had seemed depressed and meditative, had said to Sturges: " 'Oh, you are young, you are young—be glad of it: be glad of it and *live*. Live all you can: it's a mistake not to. It doesn't so much matter what you do—but live. This place makes it all come over me. I see it now. I haven't done so—and now I'm old. It's too late. It has gone past me—I've lost it. You have time. You are young. Live!' "[13]

James's letter to Howells, summer of 1901:

"Ever since receiving and reading your elegant volume of short tales—the arrival of which from you was affecting and delightful to me—I've meant to write to you, but the wish has struggled in vain with the daily distractions of a tolerably busy summer. I should blush, however, if the season were to melt away without my greeting and thanking you. I read your book with joy and found in it recalls from far far away—stray echoes and scents as from another, the American, the prehistoric existence. The thing that most took me was that entitled *A Difficult Case,* which I found beautiful and admirable, ever so true and ever so *done.* But I fear I more, almost than anything else, lost myself in mere envy of your freedom to do, and, speaking, vulgarly, to place, things of that particular and so agreeable dimension—I mean the dimension of most of the stories in the volume. It is sternly enjoined upon one here (where an agent-man does what he can for me) that everything—every hundred—above 6 or 7 thousand words is fatal to 'placing'; so that I do them of that length, with great care, art and time (much reboiling,) and then, even then, can scarcely get them worked off—published even when they've been accepted. . . . So that (though I don't know why I inflict on you these sordid groans—except that I haven't any one else to inflict them on—and the mere affront—of being unused so inordinately long—is almost intolerable) I don't feel incited in that direction. Fortunately, however, I am otherwise immersed. I lately finished a tolerably long novel, and I've written a third of another—with still another begun and two or three more subjects awaiting me thereafter like carriages drawn up at the door and horses champing their bits. And apropos of the first named of these, which is in the hands of the Harpers, I have it on my conscience to let you know that the idea of the fiction in question had its earliest origin in a circumstance mentioned to me—years ago—in respect to no less a person than yourself. At Torquay, once, our young friend Jon. Sturges came down to spend some days near me, and, lately from Paris, repeated to me five words you had said to him one day on his meeting you during a call at Whistler's. I thought the words charming—you have probably quite forgotten them; and the whole incident suggestive—so far as it was an incident; and, more than this, they presently caused me to see in them the faint vague germ, the mere point of the *start*, of a subject. I noted them, to that end, as I note everything; and years afterwards (that is three or four) the subject sprang at me, one day, out of my notebook. I don't know if it be good; at any rate it has been treated now, for whatever it is; and my point is that it had long before—it had in the very act of striking me as a germ—got away from *you* or from anything like you! had become impersonal and independent. Nevertheless your initials figure in my little note; and if you hadn't said the five words to Jonathan he wouldn't have had them (most sympathetically and interestingly) to relate, and I shouldn't have had them to work in my imagination. The moral is that you are responsible for the whole business. But I've had it, since the book was finished, much at heart to tell you so. May you carry the burden bravely!"[14]

When Howells read *The Ambassadors,* he expressed his opinion of it in his letter of April 6, 1903, to Charles Eliot Norton. After asking Norton if he had read it, he stated that he thought it "very good work." Howells added that it must appear to Norton "very improbable to find fiction" in the *North American Review,* but he then added: "Though where will you not find fiction nowadays."

In the interim between James's letter about the use of the "germ" for *The Ambassadors* and Howells' letter to Norton, Howells published in January, 1901, the review of *The Soft Side* and his article, published in 1901 and 1902, "Mr. James's *Daisy Miller,*" both of which are included in this volume. When Howells had read *The Wings of the Dove,* he wrote James a letter; and its tenor may be guessed by James's reply of December, 1902:

"Nothing more delightful, or that has touched me more closely, even to the spring of tears, has befallen me for years, literally, than to receive your beautiful letter . . . so largely and liberally anent *The Wings of the Dove.* Every word of it goes to my heart and to 'thank you' for it seems a mere grimace. The same post brought me a letter from dear John Hay, so that my measure has been full. I haven't known anything about the American 'notices,' heaven save the mark! any more than about those here (which I am told, however, have been remarkably genial;) so that I have *not* had the sense of confrontation with a public more than usually childish—I mean had it in any special way. I confess, however, that this is my chronic sense—the more than usual childishness of publics: and it is (has been,) in my mind, long since discounted, and my work definitely insists upon being independent of such phantasms and on unfolding itself wholly from its own 'innards.' Of course, in our conditions, doing anything decent is pure disinterested, unsupported, unrewarded heroism; but that's in the day's work. The *faculty of attention* has utterly vanished from the general anglo-saxon mind, extinguished at its source by the big blatant *Bayadère* of Journalism, of the newspaper and the *picture* (above all) magazine; who keeps screaming 'Look at *me*, *I* am the thing, and I only, the thing that will keep you in relation with me *all the time* without your having to attend *one minute* of the time.' If you are moved to write anything about the *W. of the D.* do something of that—it so awfully wants saying. But we live in a lovely age for literature or for any art but the mere visual. Illustrations, loud simplifications and *grossissements,* the big buildings . . . the 'mounted' play, the prose that is careful to be in the tone of, and with the distinction of a newspaper or bill-poster advertisement—these, and these only, meseems, 'stand a chance.' But why do I talk of such chances? I am melted at your reading *en famille The Sacred Fount,* which you will, I fear, have found chaff in the mouth and which is one of several things of mine, in these last years, that have paid the penalty of having been conceived only as the 'short story' that (alone, apparently) I could hope to work off somewhere (which I mainly failed of,) and then *grew* by a rank force of its own into something of which the idea had, modestly, never been to be a book. That is essentially the case with the *S. F.*, planned, like *The Spoils of Ponyton, What Maisie Knew, The Turn of the Screw,* and various others, as a story of the '8 to 10 thousand words'!! and then having accepted its bookish necessity or destiny in consequence of becoming already, at the start, 20,000, accepted it ruefully and blushingly, moreover, since, *given the tenuity of the idea,* the larger quantity of treatment hadn't been aimed at. I remember how I would have 'chucked' *The Sacred Fount* at the 15th thousand word, if in the first place I could have afforded to 'waste' 15,000, and if in the second I were not always ridden by a superstititous terror of not finishing, for finishing's and for precedent's sake, what I have begun. I am a fair coward about *dropping,* and the book, in question, I fear, is, more than anything else, a monument to that superstition. When, if it meets my eye, I say to myself, 'You know you might not have finished it,' I make the remark not in natural reproach, but, I confess, in craven relief."[15]

Howells was "moved" to write about *The Wings of the Dove*; and in January, 1903, published in *The North American Review* the article "Mr. Henry James's Later Work," which is included in this volume. As James had suggested in his letter, Howells advised the reader to "dive" for the meaning of the novels written by the master.

On March 25, 1904, Howells related to Mrs. Howells (in a diary entry made in Bath, England), that the visit he had had with James "was quite ideal in its way" and had seemed to give "great pleasure" to James. Howells remarked that James had become very stout—in fact, he was "filled out from head to foot, in a sort of *chamfered* squareness."

Four years later when James was preparing his New York Edition, the first volumes of which appeared in 1907, comments were made by Howells about the work James was doing —and, judging by a later letter to James, he feared that similar remarks made to James himself had wounded his feelings and created a rift between the two men. On April 12, 1908, Howells wrote to Charles Eliot Norton from Leghorn that he hoped to see James and that he had had a delightful letter from him. Although he had not yet seen James's new edition and had heard only impressions of it, Howells remarked that a man of sixty-eight "cannot well re-write the books of a man of" thirty-eight and that he could "imagine the risks he has taken." James was, however, "our best in so many ways that we must always own him." He then remarked that James's *Julia Bride,* which had been appearing in *Harper's,* was, as James himself would say, " 'wonderful.' " It had to Howells "the finest touch and wisest, if worldliest, wisdom."

Howells evidenced to James in his letter of August 2, 1908, his fear of having injured his friend with remarks about the prefaces and his reactions to them. After remarking that he "fancied that something" he said about James's prefaces might not have been so "wholly pleasing" as he had meant it, Howells reported that he had been reading them aloud and that they had give "us all great satisfaction." To Howells himself the most enjoyable element of them was when James rounded upon himself and took himself "to pieces" in his "self-censure."

Howells remarked that—although all the analyses were good, subtle, and wise—the one of *The American* had seemed to him "happiest." He admitted that he had found the biographies of this book, *Roderick Hudson,* and *The Portrait of a Lady* so instructive that he realized that he, as a godfather who had fancied he knew all about them, had "really known them only from their birth, and not from their conception through their gestation." Howells then recalled how James had told him while they were rowing on Fresh Pond on a Sunday afternoon what *Roderick Hudson* was to be.

Howells ended his comments about the prefaces with the opinion that James had "done a lot of good work, but nothing better than the last half of each of these prefaces." He felt also that they would enable the public to recognize what he himself had remarked to James about his work as they had sat glued to their chairs one miserably hot afternoon: that James had imagined his fiction "as whole" and had "better fulfilled a conscious intention in it than any of" his contemporaries. He then paid tribute to the courage it had taken "to do those introductions, and the toil as great;" but he added that James "must have liked doing them—or having done them."

On August 17, 1908, James replied to explain the purpose of his prefaces:

> "My actual attitude about the Lucubrations is almost only, and quite inevitably, that they make to me, for weariness; by reason of their number and extent—I've now but a couple more to write. . . . They are, in general a sort of plea for Criticism, for Discrimination, for Appreciation on other than infantile lines—as against the so almost universal Anglo-Saxon absence of these things; which tends so, in our general trade, it seems to me, to break the heart. However, I am afraid I'm too sick of the mere doing of them, and of the general strain of the effort to avoid the deadly danger of repetition, to say much to the purpose about them. They ought, collected together, none the less, to form a sort of comprehensive manual of *vademecum* for aspirants in our arduous profession. Still, it will be long before I shall want to collect them together for that purpose and furnish them with a final Preface. As for the Edition, itself, it has racked me a little that I've had to leave out so many things that would have helped to make for rather a more vivid completeness. I don't at all regret the things, pretty numerous, that I've omitted from

deep-seated preference and design; but I do a little those that are crowded out by want of space and by the rigour of the 23 vols., and 23 only, which were the condition of my being able to arrange the matter with the Scribners at all. Twenty-three do seem a fairly blatant array—and yet I rather surmise that there may have to be a couple of supplementary volumes for certain too marked omissions; such being, on the whole, detrimental to an all professedly comprehensive presentation of one's stuff. Only these, I pray God, without Prefaces! And I have even, in addition, a dim vague view of reintroducing, with a good deal of titivation and cancellation, the too-diffuse but, I somehow feel, tolerably full and good *Bostonians* of nearly a quarter of a century ago; that production never having, even to my much disciplined patience, received any sort of justice. But it will take, doubtless, a great deal of artful re-doing—and I haven't, now, had the courage or time for anything so formidable as touching and re-touching it. I feel at the same time how the series suffers commercially from its having been dropped so completely. . . .

"I could really shed salt tears of impatience and yearning to get back, after so prolonged a blocking of traffic, to too dreadfully postponed and neglected 'creative' work; an accumulated store of ideas and reachings-out for which even now dogs my brain. . . . I never have had such a sense of almost bursting, late in the day though it be, with violent and lately too much repressed creative (again!) intention."[16]

As his letters to his brother William show, James sometimes pondered over the advantages and the disadvantages of being an expatriot and of having, therefore, to more or less confine himself to the international novel which Howells so greatly applauded. Howells doubtless greatly appreciated the fact that James after *The Tragic Muse* more or less devoted himself to writing about English life and about the American in Europe.

One of the interesting nonfiction products of the period after the turn of the century was, therefore, the biography of the American sculptor and man of letters, William Wetmore Story (1819-1895), whom James had known as another expatriot in Rome. As F. W. Dupee has remarked, the biography of Story and that of Hawthorne should be viewed as the studies of two phases of American artistic life and as portrayals, with James's memoirs, of his own formation and development as an artist.[17]

On October 27, 1908, Howells commented to his friend T. S. Perry in a letter that he had not yet seen James's *William Wetmore Story and His Friends* but that he would accept what Perry had said about the book because of his faith in his judgment. Howells then recalled that he had "met Story two or three times in his later life" and had liked him and had "fostered his attempts on editors." He also recalled that he had heard, when he had been in Rome in 1864, that " 'good' Americans" speak ill of Story "because of his supposed preference for the Englishry."

The letter Howells wrote to James on February 1, 1910, serves to fill a gap in Howells' criticism of James's fiction; for this letter is concerned with *The Bostonians* which Howells had never reviewed. Howells had been reading the novel aloud to his family, and he wrote to urge James to include the book in his collection—for to omit it would be "the greatest blunder and the greatest pity." Howells asked James to be persuaded to include it, for it was "not only one of the greatest books" James had ever written "but one of the masterpieces of all fiction."

More specifically, Howells felt that the book was one of the kind that had not "been done in our time" because it was "closely woven, deep, subtle"; because it reached into worlds that he did not think James knew; and because it proved James a "citizen of the American Cosmos." James had managed every character, wrote Howells, with "masterly clearness and power" and Verena had "something absolute in her tenderness and sweetness and loveliness"—as did "Olive in her truth and precision." To Howells, James's New Yorkers were as good as his Bostonians—and beyond that compliment Howells stated he could not go. He also thought that the towns were "wonderfully suggested" and that James had gone "to the bottom of the half-frozen Cambridge mud." Although reading the book brought back to Howells "a dear yet terrible time" and although he had never thought that he had been "wanting in a sense of" James from the first, reading *The Bostonians* had made him feel that he seemed only then to "be realizing" him.[18]

Shortly after Howells had written this letter and the one about his wife's reaction to *The Tragic Muse*, Mrs. Howells died (May 6, 1910). The grief and the loneliness which Howells, now in the nadir of his career as a novelist but still a writer of "The Editor's Easy Chair," experienced are reflected in the letters he wrote to James. Howells expressed also in a letter to James on July 1, 1910, from Mayfair W, his grief about the illness of William James. He had hoped that James would visit America during the forthcoming winter but now he was grieved that the trip would be made because of William's illness. He remarked that London was not London without the possibility of seeing James and that the one reason for his being there seemed "less and less a reason." He expressed his sorrow about James's suffering; hoped that his native land would provide "a healing shelter" for him; and regretted that he could not sail home on the ship with James, who sailed on August 12th. Howells explained that he could not sail before October.

William James died on August 26, 1910, and his death was quickly followed by that of Robertson James. Henry was, therefore, the sole survivor of his original family. Of his reaction to the loss of William, who had been his harshest family critic and yet his paternal older brother, James wrote to T. S. Perry: " 'I sit heavily stricken and in darkness, for from far back in dimmest childhood he had been my ideal Elder Brother, and I still, through all the years, saw in him, even as a small timorous boy yet, my protector, my backer, my authority and my pride.' "[19] During the year James stayed in the United States after his brothers' deaths, he—as a result of the suggestion of Mrs. William James—conceived the idea of writing *A Small Boy and Others* and *Notes of a Son and Brother*.[20]

When Howells wrote James on January 7, 1911, James was still in the United States; for he did not return to England, where he was to remain, until September. In this letter Howells related his own misery of waking at two or three every morning, of drinking his "sorrow dry," and of then drugging himself, "one way or another, back to oblivion." Howells stated that he realized that he was not cheering his friend—which he wished to do—but that perhaps it would help James to know that he had "the company that misery loves." Howells added that he admitted that he was himself "somewhat comforted" when he thought of James and realized that he was "not the only wretched man"—"selfish beast" that he was.

Although James received honorary degrees in 1911 and 1912 from Harvard and from Oxford and in 1913 the Order of Merit, his English and American friends futilely hoped that he would receive the Nobel Prize.[21] On March 4, 1911, Howells wrote to Brander Matthews to relate the news contained in a letter written by Gosse which Mrs. Cadwalader Jones had forwarded to him. Gosse not only stated that the English authors had joined to get the prize for James but asked that American writers either unite with them or make a separate appeal. Howells stated that he had suggested that Mrs. Cadwalader Jones ask Sloane to try to "commit the Academy in James's favor"—and he then asked directly if Matthews could help. Stating that he knew that Matthews would do all he could, he then asked him to have President Butler write a letter representing Columbia and to get Holt to write one for the Author's Club. As we all know, these efforts were not successful; but they indicate Howells' endless support of James.

On May 9, 1911, Howells wrote to James a letter in which he stated that he was finding "greater happiness in writing than" he ever had—and he admitted that he was "clumsily leading up to the hope and belief that" James would soon be writing again. He encouraged James to do so by asserting that he still had "great things ahead" of him "to do and to enjoy doing." He then suggested that James, "pending something inventive," should write of the "literary times and places" he had lived in; and he assured James that this type of book would be "something which the editorial soul would exult to have from" him.

From Madrid, Howells wrote to James on October 15, 1911 that he and his daughter Mildred were still seeing "Touraine homesickly, as a serene, sunny expanse of Loire levels" and that their longing had been enhanced by the reading of James's *Little Tour in France* (1885), which they had purchased in the Tauchnitz edition in their hotel. Although they could hardly bear to read the book because it made them so homesick, Howells opined that James had never written "a better, a gentler, or more charming and truthful book."

In September, 1911, *The Henry James Year Book* was published in Boston; and it contained a friendly public letter to James by Howells. When a dinner was held in honor of Howells' seventy-fifth birthday in 1912, James wrote the public letter which was quoted in part in the "Preface" to this collection. When Howells wrote James on March 17, 1912, to express his appreciation, he admitted that he did not know how to acknowledge the public letter. He stated that it had almost convinced him that he had really been of some service to James—at any rate, he was going to believe that he had for this thought would give him pleasure when he wakened in the night "to the sense of what a toad" he was and had always been. James's letter, "so fully, so beautifully kind," would help eliminate also some of his "dreadful moments of self-blame"; for Howells could think that James certainly would not abuse him in his "dotage with flattery" and that he must, therefore, not be "such a worm of the earth" as he felt himself to be.

This letter, meant for the public, had, wrote Howells, brought to him "the vision of . . . days and nights in Sacramento street" when his bosom had been young and had "swelled with pride in" James's friendship and with joy in sharing—"as if it were some 'communion of saints' "—his literary ambitions. Howells also expressed his eagerness for all men to read the letter when it was published in the *North American Review*, which he felt was "alone worthy of reporting it." He stated that he was glad that the host had not read it at the dinner, for there "the best, the finest effect of it would have been lost." He made it clear, however, that no letters had been read and that all were to be published.

When James replied on March 27, 1912, to this letter, he stated that he wished that the letter had been read at the public dinner. He then discussed the general strike in England, which he feared might lead to civil war, and the woman suffrage question, which left him indifferent.[22]

When James celebrated his seventieth birthday, his English acquaintances and friends presented him a golden bowl and had Sargent paint his portrait.[23] Howells expressed his opinion of the attempt to raise money to buy furniture for James's house in celebration of this occasion and also his reaction to *Notes of a Son and Brother* in his letter of March 31, 1913, to Mrs. T. S. Perry. To Howells, it was "a mercy that scandalous attempt on poor James's delicacy was so promptly defeated!" He was horrified by the idea and was happy that he had had "no part in it." Of James's new book, which had just been published, he wrote that he had "tasted it already. Delicious."

When Howells read the paper which James had written about Mr. and Mrs. J. T. Fields—which was published in the *Atlantic Monthly*, July, 1915—[24] he wrote his friend on June 29, 1915, not only his reactions to it but also to *A Small Boy and Others* and to *Notes of a Son and Brother*. Howells had read the paper about Fields aloud to his daughter Mildred, who had visited Mrs. Fields with her father the summer before. Both father and daughter had enjoyed the material about the Fields, but Howells had found it particularly satisfactory because it had "relumed so many old faded fires, and cast, most precious of all, a tender light" on James's youth which, remarked Howells, "used to abash me with its worldly maturity."

Howells then recalled how Fields had once brought him a James story with the "question of whether he should take it" and how he himself had replied (as we have noted earlier) that he should—and "as many more by the same hand as you can get." Howells then remarked that what he had said then was exactly what young assistant editors should be saying now—but were not. He then stated that a "change has passed over things" and that he could not serialize a story of his in any American magazine—"thousands of them as they are."

Howells also recounted to James his difficulties in writing what he termed his own "miserable memoirs." Although they made him "sick," he was writing them as he had promised to do; but he intended to end them "with going off to Venice." Because he felt writing them "something awful," he wondered the more at the "grace and ease" with which James had written about his past in his "two blithe books"—*A Small Boy and Others* and *Notes of a Son and Brother*.

When World War I occurred, James busied himself to support the British cause; and finally, after much brooding and irritation because his own country did not enter the battle to preserve civilization, James became on July 26, 1915, a British citizen. Although many criticized James for renouncing his country, Howells wrote on August 7th to Brander Matthews that, although he was sorry to lose James as "an American as well as Academician," James "had full right to do as he had done." Howells added, however, that he himself would not "bow the knee to any crowned head, even poor George V. . . ."

Howells was soon, however, to lose completely his almost life-long friend; for on February 28, 1916, James died. Howells was asked to write an article about him after his death; but he did not do so because, according to Mildred Howells, "the magazine could not meet Howells' terms." Howells did, however do a review of Lubbock's collection of James's letters and he did begin to write his unfinished memoirs of James.[25] When Howells died in 1920, he was still thinking and writing about Henry James, his friend in whom he had always had so much faith and for whom he had always had a humble admiration. For James—as for many other writers—Howells had fought a crucial and critical battle.

NOTES

[1] Edel, *Henry James,* p. 272.

[2] Lubbock, ed., *Letters of Henry James,* I, 163-6; also Matthiessen, *The James Family,* pp. 507-8.

[3] Henry James, ed., *Letters of William James,* I, 298-9; also Matthiessen, *The James Family,* p. 508.

[4] Dupee, *Henry James,* p. 142.

[5] This letter and others by Howells referred to were printed in full by Mildred Howells, *Life in Letters of William Dean Howells.* Since the dates of the letters are given, they may be easily located in this publication.

[6] Quoted by Dupee, *Henry James,* p. 148.

[7] Lubbock, ed., *Letters of Henry James,* I, 230; also Matthiessen, *James Family,* pp. 509-10.

[8] Dupee, *Henry James,* pp. 142-176.

[9] Howells had also disapproved of the Zola trial, for he sided with Dreyfus.

[10] This review was reprinted in the *Literary Reviews and Essays by Henry James, ed.,* Albert Mordell.

[11] Dupee, *Henry James,* p. 204.

[12] Lubbock, ed., *Letters of Henry James,* I, 357; also Matthiessen, *James Family,* pp. 510-11.

[13] Quoted from Henry James' *Unpublished Notebook* by Matthiessen, *James Family*, pp. 511-12.

[14] Lubbock, ed., *Letters of Henry James*, I, 375-77; also in Matthiessen, *James Family*, pp. 511-12.

[15] Lubbock, ed., *Letters of Henry James*, I, 407; quoted by Matthiessen, *James Family*, pp. 513-14.

[16] Lubbock, ed., *Letters of Henry James*, II, 99-102; quoted also in Matthiessen, *James Family*, pp. 514-5.

[17] Dupee, *Henry James*, p. 24.

[18] *The Bostonians* was not included in the New York Edition because of certain editorial and publication difficulties.

[19] Quoted in Dupee, *Henry James*, p. 247.

[20] *Ibid.*, pp. 247-8.

[21] Maeterlinck, not James, received the Nobel Prize in 1911; Gerhart Hauptman, in 1912.

[22] This letter was published in Mildred Howells's collection of letters but not in Lubbock's.

[23] Dupee, *Henry James*, p. 245.

[24] Reprinted by Edel, ed., *The American Essays of Henry James.*

[25] These were reprinted by Mildred Howells: *Life in Letters of William Dean Howells* (1928).

THE TRAGIC MUSE*

Henry James is not recognizable as anything else, and must be called a novelist because there is yet no name for the literary kind he has invented, and so none for the inventor. The fatuity of the story as a story is something that must early impress the story-teller who does not live in the stone age of fiction and criticism. To spin a yarn for the yarn's sake, that is an ideal worthy of a nineteenth-century Englishman, doting in forgetfulness of the English masters and grovelling in ignorance of the Continental masters; but wholly impossible to an American of Mr. Henry James's modernity. To him it must seem like the lies swapped between men after the ladies have left the table and they are sinking deeper and deeper into their cups and growing dimmer and dimmer behind their cigars. To such a mind as his the story could never have value except as a means; it could not exist for him as an end; it could be used only illustratively; it could be the frame, not possibly the picture. But in the mean time the kind of thing he wished to do, and began to do, and has always done, amidst a stupid clamor, which still lasts, that it was not a story (of *course*, it was not a story!), had to be called a novel; and the wretched victim of the novel-habit (only a little less intellectually degraded than the still more miserable slave of the theatre-habit), who wished neither to perceive nor to reflect, but only to be acted upon by plot and incident, was lost in an endless trouble

* *Harper's New Monthly Magazine* (September, 1890).

about it. Here was a thing called a novel, written with extraordinary charm; interesting by the vigor and vivacity with which phases and situations and persons were handled in it; inviting him to the intimacy of characters divined with creative insight; making him witness of motives and emotions and experiences of the finest import; and then suddenly requiring him to be man enough to cope with the question itself; not solving it for him by a marriage or a murder, and not spoon-victualling him with a moral minced small and then thinned with milk and water, and familiarly flavored with sentimentality or religiosity. We can imagine the sort of shame with which such a writer, so original and so clear-sighted, may sometimes have been tempted by the outcry of the nurslings of fable, to give them of the diet on which they had been pampered to imbecility; or to call together his characters for a sort of round-up in the last chapter.

The round-up was once the necessary close of every novel, as it is of every season on a Western cattle ranch; and each personage was summoned to be distinctly branded with his appropriate destiny, so that the reader need be in no doubt about him evermore. The formality received its most typical observance in *The Vicar of Wakefield*, perhaps, where the modern lover of that loveliest prospect of eighteenth-century life is amused by the conscientiousness with which fate is distributed, and vice punished and virtue rewarded. It is most distinctly honored in the breach in that charming prospect of nineteenth-century life, *The Tragic Muse*, a novel which marks the farthest departure from the old ideal of the novel. No one is obviously led to the altar; no one is relaxed to the secular arm and burnt at the stake. Vice is disposed of with a gay shrug; virtue is rewarded by innuendo. All this leaves us pleasantly thinking of all that has happened before, and asking, Was Gabriel Nash vice? Was Mrs. Dallow virtue? Or was neither either? In the nineteenth century, especially now toward the close of it, one is never quite sure about vice and virtue: they fade wonderfully into and out of each other; they mix, and seem to stay mixed, at least around the edges.

Mr. James owns that he is himself puzzled by the extreme actuality of his facts; fate is still in solution, destiny is not precipitated; the people are still going uncertainly on as we find people going on in the world about us all the time. But that does not prevent our being satisfied with the study of each as we find it in the atelier of a master. Why in the world should it? What can it possibly matter that Nick Dormer and Mrs. Dormer are not certainly married, or that Biddy Dormer and Sherringham certainly are? The marriage or the non-marriage cannot throw any new light on their characters; and the question never was what they were going to do, but what they were. This is the question that is most sufficiently if not distinctly answered. They never wholly emerge from the background which is a condition of their form and color; and it is childish, it is Central African, to demand that they shall do so. It is still more Central African to demand such a thing in the case of such a wonderful creature as Gabriel Nash, whose very essence is elusiveness; the lightest, slightest, airiest film of personality whose insubstantiality was ever caught by art; and yet so strictly of his time, his country, his kind. He is one sort of modern Englishman; you are as sure of that as you are of the histrionic type, the histrionic character, realized in the magnificent full-length of Miriam Rooth. *There* is mastery for you! There is the woman of the theatre, destined to the stage from her cradle: touched by family, by society, by love, by friendship, but never swayed for a moment from her destiny, such as it is, the tinsel glory of triumphing for a hundred nights in the same part. An honest creature, most thoroughly honest in heart and act, and most herself when her whole nature is straining toward the realization of some one else; vulgar, sublime; ready to make any sacrifice for her art, to "toil terribly," to suffer everything for it, but perfectly aware of its limitations at its best, while she provisionally contents herself with its second-best, she is by all odds so much more perfectly presented in *The Tragic Muse* than any other like woman in fiction, that she seems the only woman of the kind ever presented in fiction.

As we think back over our year's pleasure in the story (for we will own we read it serially as it was first printed), we have rather a dismaying sense of its manifold excellence; dismaying, that is, for a reviewer still haunted by the ghost of the duty of cataloguing a book's merits. While this ghost walks the Study, we call to mind that admirable old French actress of whom Miriam gets her first lessons; we call to mind Mrs. Rooth, with her tawdry scruples; Lady Dormer, with her honest English selfishness; Mrs. Dallow, with her awful good sense and narrow high life and relentless will; Nick's lovely sister Biddy and unlovely sister Grace; Nick himself, with his self-devotion to his indefinite future; Sherringham, so good and brave and sensible and martyred; Dashwood, the born man of the theatre, as Miriam is the born woman; and we find nothing caricatured or overcharged, nothing feebly touched or falsely stated. As for the literature, what grace, what strength! The style is a sweetness on the tongue, a music in the ear. The whole picture of life is a vision of London aspects such as no Englishman has yet been able to give: so fine, so broad, so absolute, so freed from all necessities of reserve or falsity.

Its modernity, its recognition of the very latest facts of society and art, and of that queer flirtation between them that can never be a marriage, is one of the very most valuable, most delightful things about the book. Modernity, indeed, is always somehow a charming thing when you get it skilfully expressed in a picture or a story. . . .

HENRY JAMES*

I came to a knowledge of Mr. Henry James's wonderful workmanship in the first manuscript of his that passed through my hands as sub-editor. I fell in love with it instantly, and I have never ceased to delight in that exquisite artistry. I have read all that he has written, and I have never read anything of his without an ecstatic pleasure in his unrivaled touch. In literary handling no one who has written fiction in our language can approach him, and his work has shown an ever-deepening insight. I have my reserves to certain things of his; if hard pressed I might even undertake to better him here and there, but after I had done that I doubt if I should like him so well. In fact, I prefer to let him alone, to take him for what he is in himself, and to be grateful for every new thing that comes from his pen. I will not try to say why his works take me so much; that is no part of my business in these papers, and I can understand why other people are not taken at all with him, for no reason that they can give, either. At the same time, I have no patience with them, and but small regard for their taste.

* From Howells' *My Literary Passions* (1895).

James's

TERMINATIONS

and George Moore's

CELIBATES*

I do not know any book more thoroughly characteristic of the author than Terminations. Mr. James has written many other books which represent him more fully, more strenuously, more intensely, or how you will, but none, I believe, in which you taste more distinctly his peculiar quality. This, I think, has grown constantly finer in all that he has written of later years, more delicate, more exquisite; and in Terminations, where it is as pervasive as a perfume, it has its finest expression. The things for the most part end vaguely, diffusing themselves and ceasing upon the sense without insistence upon a definite intention, and this is to my mind one of their rarest charms and the subtlest proofs of their unrivalled artistry. An impression of harmonious beauty is what remains with you.

There is rather more humor in the working out of the pathetic conceptions than the author commonly permits himself. But the conceptions of the stories are all pathetic, and the humor is the break of a reluctant and hopeless laugh from the irremediable and inconsolable melancholy of the situation.

* *Harper's Weekly* (July 27, 1895).

There is scarcely a smile in the sketch called The Altar of the Dead, and scarcely more in The Middle Years, but in The Death of the Lion, and The Coxon Fund, the laugh comes in again and again. It is hard to say which of the humorous motives in the last is the most delicious: the great intellectual fraud Saltram, who was made to live upon such generous victims as the Kent Mulvilles, or the Kent Mulvilles, who were made for such frauds to live upon; the vulgar, self-satisfied selfishness of Gravener, put to torment by having to break with his American betrothed because she has lost her money; or the contrast of her Bostonian idealism with his practical, necessary British egotism; but it is all immensely funny and immensely sad.

It is the only one of the studies in which American character is introduced, and I think this a pity, for in a certain sort of it no one's touch is so brilliant and secure as Mr. James's. He consoles one a little for its absence in The Middle Years and The Death of the Lion by dealing with the literary life, where he is so easily first that I think there is no second. Neither of these pieces is so rich and full as The Lesson of the Master (forever admirable and insurpassable) or The Author of Beltraffio; but each has the finer graces of those masterpieces; and each reflects a different phase of that life with matchless and unerring charm. The successful author hunted down by relentless social recognition, and literally done to death by the pursuit of a philistine and pitiless hospitality, and the defeated author dying in the arms of his one most magnanimous adorer; these are suggested with a touching humor which would abhor the crude excess of my statement.

Everywhere the admirable book is marked by a wise and sensitive reticence, which sometimes shades into the defect of its virtue, perhaps; but I am not sure of this. It is all in the minor key, but it is full of a distinction which is hard to preserve in the effects of pathos, whether it is the pathos that weeps or the pathos that laughs. The first is so easily maudlin, the last is so easily sardonic, but neither is imaginable of Mr. James, whose appeals to the sympathy of his reader are never such as to involve a loss of self-respect with the most responsive. One quits his company pensive with the sense of life which has been lived, and will be lived again and again.

II

If pathos is the dominant note of Terminations, tragedy is that of Celibates. I confess that whatever I might say of the difference in such pleasures, I have found nearly as much pleasure in Mr. Moore's studies as in Mr. James's. But I am by no means disposed to undervalue Mr. Moore's in comparison, for I find there the work of a very great talent. I suppose that I did not come to a just sense of this talent until I had read Esther Waters, and I hope I have not now the superabounding zeal of the new convert. For a long time it seemed to me that Mr. Moore was simply trying to do the Zola act, though I did not so much object to the act as to the fact that Zola had already done it. But I must own that Esther Waters gave me a feeling of his power, of his original force, which I had not had till I read that very strong novel, that mainly just, mainly right-minded book. Of course, there are leaks in nearly everything, and the story will not hold praise at every point; one might convict it of errors of taste, even errors of propriety, but it is worlds better than anything else English (always excepting Mr. Hardy), and one must in gratitude and conscience put it with the continental works of fiction which are also works of art. While Mr. Moore lives, indeed, one must never despair of English fiction, for there is distinctly a hope for it, and a great hope, in him.

Esther Waters was not a book to put in a young girl's hands, because though not immoral it was not wholly decent, as certain well-known facts of life are not; and as regards the young girl, fiction must be

"Content to dwell in decencies forever,"

or not be for her, no matter how moral, how disciplinary it may be. For the same reason Celibates must be withheld from those whose innocence is dear. The book could not do them harm, but its bold knowledge might leave a stain in the mind, and so it is better to withhold it.

As to harm, perhaps it might even do good rather, if it could be risked, as it cannot. I feel quite sure that there is a lesson in Miss Lawson's career, as it is portrayed in the first and longest of the studies, which it is a pity the Miss Lawsons should not learn, if they are capable of learning anything. It is at any rate a spectacle of the hateful passion for power, which those not possessed with it can no doubt best profit by. It will be a question with casuists to the end whether the girl's lust of conquest was so much better than the other lust which could never sway her from her self-control. She is a detestable creature, and though she remains "pure" through all the risks she takes to make her lovers feel her charm, it is doubtful whether she remains better than the worst in what M. Bourget would call her "chaste depravity." She is realized to the reader with a sort of cold distinctness which is very remarkable, and after he has followed her to the defeat which such conquests as hers must always end in, he has a sense of her character, almost of her presence, such as the types of fiction seldom leave.

It seems to be rather Mr. Moore's special gift, in this book at least, to present his women so clearly that you seem to have met them. This is the case even with such an illusive personality as Kitty Hare's in the story of John Norton, and it is most triumphantly so with Mrs. Lahens in the piteous tragedy of

Agnes Lahens. The vulgarity of the mother's beauty haunts the inner eye long after the book is shut, and doubtless the heart-break in the story would not be so terrible without it.

One must leave to the reader such slight story as these things involve. What gives them importance is their naked truth, which is very, very naked now and then. Sometimes the nakedness abashes, sometimes it appalls, as in that horrible divination and recognition of John Norton's, where, confronted with the "ignominy of life," he perceives that his passion and the tramp's violence are from the same instinct. This is the ascetic's sense of it, and it is not the less poignantly cruel because there is other truth concerning the fact. It is curious that in dealing with a thing of such nightmare hideousness as Kitty Hare's fate, the author finds himself on the plane of the ideal more than in any other passage of his book. He has wholly to imagine the fact as it exists in her consciousness, and it must be owned that he imagines it with extraordinary power. The immense, the hopeless pity of it surpasses even the horror.

In the pathos of Agnes Lahens's case he is more merciful, though he is scarcely less moving. The fate of the innocent girl who comes home from her convent to such a half-caste social and intellectual world as surrounds her painted mother with its fetid atmosphere is for the moment terrible, but she escapes from it to the quiet of the convent again, and you have only the pang of her past suffering when you think of her, but for Kitty Hare's blighted purity and for John Norton's sense of "the ignominy of life," you perceive that there is no consolation but death.

Mr. Moore likes to employ the grand means of moving his reader, now and then, but I think his talent is shown less in such feats than in the marvellous accuracy of the impression he strikes of such types, men and women, as form the circle of Mrs. Lahens. The moral deadness which characterizes that circle is something that has never before been so fully shown in literature, though it has long been known in the world, and has its counterpart, more or less distinct, everywhere.

The perfection of the writer's art convinces you of his fidelity in this study and in that of the franker brutalities of Bohemia in Paris. No one has yet painted English life of the present day so well as Mr. James, in certain of its phases; in certain other phases none so well as Mr. Moore. This is what you find yourself saying whether you know it very well at first hand or not; for, as I have suggested, the excellence of art persuades of truth. It is all the more interesting then, to find Mr. Moore employing so largely in these stories the analytical method which Mr. James has perfected. It is his, and any one's, as well as Mr. James's, but no one can now use it without making the reader think of Mr. James.

Doubtless it is to this method that both the books I have been speaking owe the peculiar property of their several studies, or stories, or sketches. In each of these there is the nutritive substance of a whole novel: not a great novel, of course, but the ordinary novel of commerce; though this again requires qualification, for it seems insufficient praise. In any case, however, I confidently commend them to people who have not the time for novels, or the taste for new Spanish plays. For my own pleasure I could wish that there were at once a score of books like these two.*

* When George Moore published *Confessions of a Young Man* (1886) in England, he included in it some pages about Henry James in which he also made some disparaging comments about Howells. He stated that he had purchased some three or four of Howells' novels and had found them overflowing with girls in white dresses; languid mothers; mild witticisms; and young men who were cynical or a little overshadowed by love—in a word, a Tom Robertson comedy spiced with American. Moore wrote that he said to himself: "Henry James went to France and read Tourgueneff. W. D. Howells stayed at home and read Henry James." To this remark he added that Henry James's mind was of a higher cast, that James sought to follow Turgenev in writing the moral history of his native country, and that to do so he borrowed at first hand—and knew what he was borrowing. Howells, however, borrowed at second hand—and did not understand what he was borrowing.

Although Howells might have read these insulting remarks which Moore made, it is doubtful that he did so in view of the glowing comments which he made about Moore's work in his review of 1895. Since Moore's indictment of Howells has often been repeated, I should like to quote here the defense I made of Howells in *Literary Reviews and Essays by Henry James* and also the remark Howells made to me in a letter about Moore's remark. In the volume of essays and reviews of Henry James which I edited, I wrote (page 327):

> "Howells did not stay at home; he had been in Europe in the sixties before James began his career as a story writer. Howells was not an imitator of James, as Moore implies. Still, again as Howells tells us, in the middle seventies he was a devout reader of Turgenev, reading most of his books many times over. And in that period James had written only one novel which Howells accepted for the Atlantic Monthly, and he himself had published several novels before *Roderick Hudson*."

Howells made the following comment in his letter to me of May 2, 1916 (which I quote with the permission of the Howells' estate) about Moore's comment: "He [Moore] had so long been a brilliant expatriate in Paris that he felt obliged to prove his familiarity with continental literature by insulting our own."

THE SOFT SIDE*

"It seems to me the great fault of our manners, when we have them," said the Easy Chair, "is that they are personal and occasional manners. These, when they are good, are very good, but when they are bad they make you wish that the person's behavior was governed by a convention or a tradition of breeding which prescribed a certain type of conduct, not to be varied at will. That was the old ideal; but no Americans now have any ideal of politeness except the colored Americans. They seem really to love good manners, though perhaps they sometimes value them beyond good morals."

"But they are always delightful!"

"Yes, and no doubt their morals are better than they would be if their manners were bad. But I believe, of course," said the Easy Chair, rising on the wings of optimism again, "the actual state is merely transitional. We have no manners because we are waiting to get the best; and there is a play of rudeness in our life which is no real reflection of our character. But we must not wait too long! Manners are one of the most precious heritages from the past. We may disuse forms, but we must not disuse forms a great while. Goodness of heart, purity of morals, show themselves in forms, and practically do not exist without them. Forms in conduct are like forms in art. They alone can express manners; and they are built slowly, painfully, from the thought, the experience, of the whole race. In literature, for instance, they alone can impart the sense of style; they alone represent authority—"

* *Harper's Monthly Magazine* (January, 1901).

The words of the Easy Chair lost themselves in an inarticulate murmur, but with the last the editor was reminded of something that seemed quite in the line of its thinking. It was something that a woman had said of Mr. Henry James's latest collection of his stories, which for reasons of his own he calls *The Soft Side*. "When you read most books," she said, "you feel merely that you are reading a book. But when you read a book of Henry James's you feel that you are reading *an author.*"

She had a right to speak, for she was one of those devoted adherents of his who have read him from the beginning, and who alone are perfectly in his secret: not that they can always tell it! Perhaps she was the more devoted because so many women, of the sort that would rather be flattered than interpreted, are impatient of this master's work, and she wished to distinguish herself from them. In the talk that followed she was not very intelligible, though she was voluble enough, as to what in a writer imparted the sense of authorship; and the editor was left wondering whether it might not be a writer's power of getting at himself. Of course he would have to be of a quality worth getting at, but writers of inferior quality are so much and so finally on the surface that the fact of an author ever getting below it would itself be proof of his quality; and it seemed to him that of all the authors now writing English Mr. James had supremely this gift. It might be said in his reproach, but not by any critic worth while, that he was sometimes so subliminal that he was scarcely on the surface at all. "One may very well penetrate the depths below," this sort of critic might urge, "but why pull the hole in after one?" This would be the worst he could say, however, and how much he would then leave unsaid! It is not merely that Mr. James has supremely the gift of getting at himself, but that when he has got there he has arrived at a view of life such as no one else has framed; and his method of representing life, of making the reader share his view, is of a nature as delicate as it is peculiar. If we could imagine the perfume of a flower without the flower, the bouquet of wine without the wine, we should have something suggestive of the effect of his fiction with the sympathetic intelligence. In this last book of his there are certain pieces—like "The Great Condition," "In Europe," "Paste," "The Abasement of the Northmores," and "John Delavoy," to name no others—which are so captivatingly final in their way that one could not imagine anything better, or if there were anything better, could not desire it. No author has more fully perfected his method; but his control of the sympathetic intelligence is so absolute that this does not concern itself with the method, and is only in too much danger of forgetting it, of ignoring the consummate art, in the joyous sense of the life portrayed. Not since English began to be written has it so clearly embodied a literary intention of such refinement, or so unerringly imparted a feeling of character. In a time when the miasms of a gross and palpable fable are thick about us, this exquisite air breathes like a memory and a prophecy of days when fiction was and shall be valued for beauty and distinction. Here, aesthetically, are the good manners, the best manners, the form of the great world, the fashion of the modernity which is of all times, and to this school young aspirants may come to learn the art of being one's self from a master who is never more himself than when he is making you forget him.

MR. JAMES'S DAISY MILLER *

As I have noted before in these papers, it is the fate of most novelists to be associated in the minds of readers with a certain type of heroine, or with a single heroine. If it is a type that represents the novelist he is not unfairly used; for the type may be varied into distinctive characters; if it is a single character it seems not so just, for every novelist has invented many characters. Mr. Henry James, for instance, has given us more, and more finely, yet strongly, differenced heroines than any novelist of his time, but at the mention of his name a single creation of his will comes so prominently to mind that Daisy Miller will for the moment make us forget all her sisters.

I

Mr. James's time is still ours, and while perfect artistry is prized in literature, it is likely to be prolonged indefinitely beyond our time. But he belongs pre-eminently to that period following the Civil War when our authorship felt the rising tide of national life in an impulse to work of the highest refinement, the most essential truth. The tendency was then toward a subtle beauty, which he more than any other American writer has expressed in his form, and toward a keen, humorous, penetrating self-criticism, which seized with joy upon the expanding national life, and made it the material of fiction as truly national as any yet known. Mr. J. W. De Forest

* *Harper's Bazaar* (January, 1902); published also in *Heroines of Fiction* (1901).

was the pioneer in the path which the American novelists were to take; and hard upon him came Mr. Henry James, as unlike him as one talent could well be unlike another, and yet of the same mission in preparing the way, and planting the seeds of an imaginative literature, native to our soil, but taking the four winds of heaven in its boughs. They were as like in their equipment, through study and sojourn abroad, as they have been unlike in their destiny. Mr. De Forest's books are a part of our literary history; Mr. James's books are a part of our literature. Mr. De Forest somehow offended "the finer female sense," in whose favor the prosperity of our fiction resides, and he is no longer read; Mr. James, who flattered it as little, lastingly piqued it, and to read him if for nothing but to condemn him is the high intellectual experience of the daughters of mothers whose indignant girlhood resented while it adored his portraits of American women. To enjoy his work, to feel its rare excellence, both in conception and expression is a brevet of intellectual good form while the women who have it prize at all its worth. This is not a history of American fiction, and I cannot arrange here for giving Mr. James even a provisional predominance in it; but those who know our short and simple annals, in that sort, will no doubt place him where he belongs. Those who do not know them may at least be told that no American writer has been more the envy and ambition of generous youth trying for distinction as well as sincerity in their work.

II

Mr. James is not quite the inventor of the international novel, as I intimated in my notices of "The Initials," but he is the inventor, beyond question, of the international American girl. He recognized and portrayed the innocently adventuring, unconsciously periculant American maiden, who hastened to efface herself almost as soon as she saw herself in that still flattering if a little mocking mirror, so that between two sojourns in Europe, a decade apart, she had time to fade from the vision of the friendly spectator. In 1860-70, you saw her and heard her everywhere on the European continent; in 1870-80, you sought her in vain amidst the monuments of art, or on the misty mountaintops, or at the tables d'hote. Her passing might have been the effect of a more instructed civilization, or it might have been a spontaneous and voluntary disappearance. In any case she was gone, and it seemed a pity, for she was sweet, and harmless, with a charm derived from our earth and sky, a flavor of new-world conditions imparting its wilding fragrance to that strange environment as freely as to its native air. I could well fancy her discoverer feeling a pang of desolation to find no longer in the living world this lovely creature, who perished as it were of her own impossibility, and whose faded ghost has no habitat but in his faithful page.

It was perhaps in some such divine despair that he left the field of international fiction, which he has made his own, and had kept for so many years, and turned to English life, with only a thin American presence flitting now and then across the scene. He has done better work, because maturer work, in the treatment of this alien material than he did in the earlier fiction before he possessed himself of the international field. His English people have the convincing effect of having been more truly seen than others except Trollope's, but they are not those absolute contributions to polite learning which his internationals are. No one else could do them; certainly no living Englishman; and yet no one resents the author's late preoccupation with them, and demands his return to the types of that Atlantis, psychologically midway between Europe and America, where his art ripened and perfected itself in the study of character which confided its existence to him earliest if not onlyest. One demands this of him with a strong disposition to implore him, if the demand fails, to comply in the interest of history, which must, without his help, fail of some of the most curious and interesting, not to say significant, phases of modern civilization.

Since he began to note Americo-European manners, we have gone increasingly abroad, and his field has indefinitely broadened, and filled itself with an increasing variety of figures. If these have lost the refreshing sharpness of outline which first tempted his eye, they have gained in a fine differentiation which ought still more sympathetically to invite his subtle fancy. A whole new generation has grown up in the international field, and since he abandoned it, no one else has held it in any such force as to be able to dispute his sovereignty if he should come back to it.

III

It is a curious and interesting fact of Mr. James's literary fortunes that in his short stories—one is obliged to call them stories for want of a more closely fitting word—rather than his more extended fictions are the heroes and the heroines we know him best by. He has the art of so environing the slightest presentment of female motive that it shows life-size in the narrow space of a sketch or study; and you remember such a picture with a fullness of detail and a particularity wanting to many colossal figures. You seem in the retrospect to have lived a long time with the pictures, looks, attitudes; phrases remain with you; and when you revert to the book you do not lose this sense of rich amplitude. It would be futile to catalogue the personalities which are so real in the recollection of stories so numerous but not half numerous enough; and it is only for the pleasure of naming them over that I mention at random Mrs. Hedway in "The Siege of London," the terrible Georgina in "Georgina's Reasons," Madame Mauve in the story called after her, Pandora in "Pandora," Lady Barbarina in "Lady Barbarina Lemon," that pathetic presence in "The Altar of the Dead," the two wives of the master in "The Lesson of the Master," both the girls in "The Spoils of Poynton," the heroine, and Mrs. Dallow, the sub-heroine, in "The Tragic Muse," the daughter in "Marriages," the poor, shabbily defrauded girl in "The Third Person," Lily in "Miss Gunton of Poughkeepsie." The list is inexhaustible, and it is not only futile but dangerous to deal with it, for your forgetfulness of any figure accuses your taste in all the rest, and if you leave out a general favorite you are in peril of falling a prey to the furious resentment of those who adore just that neglected heroine.

No other novelist has approached Mr. James in his appreciation of women, and in his ability to suggest the charm which is never wholly absent from women, whether they are good, bad or indifferent in looks or behavior. Take all the other men that have written novels in English and match their women with his, and they seem not to have written of women at all. A few women may vie with him in the portrayal of a few figures; Jane Austen may, and Fanny Burney, and Miss Edgeworth, and George Eliot, and the Brontes, and Mrs. Humphry Ward; but their heroines are as much outnumbered by his as the novelists are in every other way surpassed. The fact is not affected by the want of general recognition; it is not yet known to the ignorant masses of educated people that Mr. James is one of the greatest masters of fiction who has ever lived. It is because he has worked in a fashion of his own, in regions of inquiry not traversed by the herd of adventurers, and dealt with material not exploited before that he is still to the critical Jews a stumbling-block and to the critical Greeks foolishness. But time will inevitably care for this unrivalled artist, or this unique psychologist who deals artist-wise with his knowledge of human nature; and he will yet take that eminent place for which he has no rival.

I cannot, in thinking of him and his somewhat baffling failure of immediate acceptance, promise myself that his right will be acknowledged soon; his own generation, in its superior refinement, was better fitted to appreciate him than the present period coarsened and vulgarized by the prevalence of puerile romance; and yet if his earliest masterpiece had been offered to this thicker-witted time, I doubt if it would have suffered the same injustice which it met from a more enlightened tribunal, or at least the same kind of injustice. It is pathetic to remember how "Daisy Miller" was received, or rather rejected, as an attack on American girlhood, and yet is so perfectly intelligible that it should have been taken so by Americans who had still a country to be so inclusively proud of that they could not bear the shadow of question to fall upon any phase of it. Our political descent to the European level has not only thickened our skins but it has in a manner so broadened, though it has imbruted our minds, that if she could have come again we should see Daisy Miller's innocent freedom in the face of immemorial convention with the liberal and tolerant pleasure which the English at once felt in it. We should not be blinded to her charm, or to the subtile patriotism which divined and portrayed it, by a patriotism which, if fervent and generous, was not so subtile as the author's. But as I have said, Daisy Miller cannot come again. The very conditions that would render us patient of her now have rendered her impossibility impossible. It is a melancholy paradox, but we need not be inconsolable, for though she has perished forever from the world, we have her spiritual reflex still vivid in the sensitive mirror which caught with such accuracy her girlish personality while it still walked the earth in the dusty ways of European travel.

IV

The story of Daisy Miller is as slight as Mr. James delights to make the frame of his picture, which depends so very little for its quality upon the frame. She is first seen at Vevey in Switzerland, with her young but terribly mature little brother and their mother, a little, lonely American group in the rather impertinent custody of a courier whom they make their domestic if not social equal; and she is seen last at Rome (where indeed she dies of the fever) the wonder of the international and the opprobrium of the compatriotic society. Such drama as arises from the simple circumstances precipitates itself in a few spare incidents which, in the retrospect, dwindle to nothing before the superior interest of the psychology. A girl of the later eighteen-seventies, sent with such a mother as hers to Europe by a father who remains making money in Schenectady, after no more experience of the world than she got in her native town, and at a number of cultivated but not rude, reckless but not bold, inexpugnably ignorant of the conventionally right, and spiritedly resentful of control by criterions that offend her own sense of things, she goes about Europe doing exactly what she would do at home, from an innocence as guileless as that which shaped her conduct in her native town. She knows no harm and she means none; she loves life, and talking, and singing, and dancing, and "attentions," but she is no flirt, and she is essentially and infinitely far from worse. Her whole career, as the reader is acquainted with it, is seen through the privity of the young Europeanized American who meets her at Vevey and follows her to Rome in a fascination which they have for each other, but which is never explicitly a passion. This side of the affair is of course managed with the fine adroitness of Mr. James's mastery; from the first moment the sense of their potential love is a delicate pleasure for the reader, till at the last it is a delicate pang, when the girl has run her wild gantlet and is dead not only of the Roman fever but of the blows dealt her in her course. There is a curious sort of fatality in it all. She is destined by innate and acquired indiscipline to do the things she does; and she is not the less doomed to suffer the things she suffers. In proportion to the offence she gives by her lawless innocence the things she does are slight things, but their consequence breaks her heart, and leave the reader's aching, as Winterbourne's must have ached life-long.

V

The young man is sitting in the garden of the Trois Couronnes, at Vevey, talking with her terrible little brother, when Daisy Miller comes down the walk toward them. "She was dressed in white muslin, with a hundred frills and flounces, and knots of pale-colored ribbon. She was bareheaded, but she balanced in her hand a large parasol, with a deep border of embroidery, and she was strikingly, admirably pretty. . . . He was ceasing to be embarrassed, for he had begun to perceive that she was not the least embarrassed herself. . . . She gradually gave him more of the benefit of her glance; and then he saw that this glance was perfectly direct and unshrinking. It was not, however, what would have been called an immodest glance, for the young girl's eyes were singularly honest and fresh. They were wonderfully pretty eyes; and, indeed, Winterbourne had not seen for a long time anything prettier than his fair country-woman's various features—her complexion, her nose, her ears, her teeth. . . . As regards this young lady's face he made several observations. It was not at all insipid, but it was not exactly expressive; and though it was eminently delicate, Winterbourne mentally accused it—very forgivingly —of a want of finish. He thought it very possible that Master Randolph's sister was a coquette; he was sure she had a spirit of her own; but in her bright, sweet, superficial little visage there was no mockery, no irony." Before long it became obvious that she was much disposed to conversation—having first assured herself that he was "a real American." "Her lips and her eyes were constantly moving. She had a soft, slender, agreeable voice, . . . with all her prettiness in her lively eyes, and in her light, slightly monotonous smile."

Before the end of the day, her mother has evasively appeared and been unwillingly made acquainted with her daughter's unknown friend, whom the girl has already easily made invite her to go with him to see the castle of Chillon. The mother is not surprised, that evening, in the same garden, when Daisy tells him she wishes he would take her a row on the lake. Mrs. Miller sees no social objection, but suggests, "I should think you had better find out what time it is." The courier, however, who has arrived to announce that Randolph has gone to bed, ventures to interpose. " 'I suppose you don't think it's proper!' Daisy exclaimed. . . . 'Oh, I hoped you would make a fuss. I don't care to go, now.' 'I myself shall make a fuss if you don't go,' said Winterbourne. 'That's all I want—a fuss,' and the young girl began to laugh again. . . . Daisy turned away from Winterbourne, looking at him, smiling, and fanning herself. 'Good-night,' she said, 'I hope you are disappointed, or disgusted, or something!' He looked at her, taking the hand she offered. 'I am puzzled,' he answered. 'Well, I hope it won't keep you awake.' "

I should not know where else to find the witless purposelessness—beyond the moment's excitement and the pleasure of bewildering a young man—in much of a girl's behavior more sufficiently yet more sparingly suggestive than in those admirable passages. The girl is a little fool, of course, but while her youth lasts she is an angelic, a divine fool, with caprices that have the quality of inspirations. She behaves at Vevey with Winterbourne, "a real American," as she would have done with a "gentleman friend" at Schenectady. He meets her at the house of a Europeanized American lady who would fain Europeanize Daisy enough at least to save her from scandal. "Daisy was exchanging greetings very prettily with her hostess;

but when she heard Winterbourne's voice she quickly turned her head. 'Well, I declare!' she said. 'I told you I should come,' Winterbourne rejoined smiling. 'Well, I didn't believe it,' said Miss Daisy. . . . 'You might have come to see me!' 'I arrived only yesterday.' 'I don't believe that,' the young girl declared. . . . 'Why, you were awfully mean at Vevey. You wouldn't do anything. You wouldn't stay there when I asked you.' 'My dearest young lady,' cried Winterbourne with eloquence, 'have I come all the way to Rome to encounter your reproaches?' 'Just hear him say that!' said Daisy, giving a twist to a bow on Mrs. Walker's dress. 'Did you ever hear anything so quaint?' 'So quaint, my dear?' murmured Mrs. Walker, in the tone of a partisan of Winterbourne. 'Well, I don't know,' said Daisy, fingering Mrs. Walker's ribbons. 'Mrs. Walker, I want to tell you something! . . . You know I'm coming to your party. . . . But I want your permission to bring a friend. . . . It's an intimate friend of mine—Mr. Giovanelli,' said Daisy, without a tremor in her clear little voice, or a shadow on her brilliant little face. . . . 'He's an Italian; . . . he's the handsomest man in the world except Mr. Winterbourne! . . . He thinks ever so much of Americans. He's tremendously clever. He's perfectly lovely!' "

The afternoon before the party Mrs. Walker and Winterbourne find Daisy walking on the Pincio, at the supreme hour of the promenade, with Giovanelli, quite as she would have been with a "gentleman friend" at home. Mrs. Walker wants her to leave him and get into her carriage, but Daisy thinks it would disappoint and wound him, and she will not do that. In the evening she comes to the party long after her mother has appeared, and comes alone with Giovanelli, as she might with a "gentleman friend" in Schenectady. When she goes up to take leave of her hostess, Mrs. Walker turns her back on her. It is the beginning of the end, in which all society turns its back on Daisy.

Winterbourne sees her for the last time in the Colosseum at midnight, alone with Giovanelli. " 'How long have you been here?' he asked almost brutally. Daisy, lovely in the flattering moonlight, looked at him a moment. Then, 'All the evening,' she answered, gently. 'I never saw anything so pretty.' 'I am afraid that you will not think Roman fever very pretty. This is the way people catch it.'. . . 'I never was sick,' the girl declared. 'I don't look like much, but I'm healthy! I was bound to see the Colosseum by moonlight; I shouldn't have wanted to go home without that; and we've had the most beautiful time, haven't we, Mr. Giovanelli?'. . . 'I should advise you,' said Winterbourne, 'to drive home as fast as possible.' 'What you say is very wise,' Giovanelli rejoined. 'I will go and make sure that the carriage is at hand.'. . . Daisy followed Winterbourne. He kept looking at her; she seemed not the least embarrassed. . . . Then noticing his silence, she asked him why he did not speak. . . . He only began to laugh. They passed under one of the dark archways; Giovanelli was in front with the carriage. Here Daisy stopped a moment, looking at the young American. '*Did* you believe, the other day, I was engaged?'. . . 'I believe it makes very little difference whether you are engaged or not!' He felt the young girl's pretty eyes fixed upon him through the thick gloom of the archway. . . . 'I don't care,' said Daisy, in a little strange tone, 'whether I have the Roman fever or not.' "

In her delirium she entreats her mother to tell Winterbourne that she never was engaged to Giovanelli. After her death he finds himself alone with the Italian by her grave. "He seemed to wish to say something. At last he said, 'She was the most beautiful young lady I ever saw, and the most amiable,' and then he added, 'and she was the most innocent.' "

VI

The perfection of the workmanship in this little book

could not be represented without an apparent exaggeration which would wrong its scrupulous but most sufficient expression. If no word could be spared without in some degree spoiling it, none could be added without cumbering its beauty with a vain decoration. To quote from it at all is to wish to quote it all; and one resigns one's self the more easily to the impossibility of giving a notion of the perfection of the performance in view of the impossibility of imparting a due sense, at second hand, of the loveliness and truth of the conception.

The reader must go to the book for both, and when he has read it I think he will agree with me that never was any civilization offered a more precious tribute than that which a great artist paid ours in the character of Daisy Miller. But our civilization could not imagine the sincerity in which the tribute was offered. It could not realize that Daisy Miller was presented in her divine innocence, her inextinguishable trust in herself and others, as the supreme effect of the American attitude toward womanhood. The American man might have suffered her—perhaps more than suffered her; pitied her; adored her even—but the American woman would none of her. She fancied in the poor girl a libel of her nationality, almost a libel of her sex, and failed to seize her wilding charm, her flowerlike purity. The American woman would none of Daisy Miller, not because the American woman was ungracious or ungrateful, but because she was too jealous of her own perfection to allow that innocence might be reckless, and angels in their ignorance of evil might not behave as discreetly as worse people.

MR. HENRY JAMES'S LATER WORK *

It has been Mr. James's lot from the beginning to be matter of unusually lively dispute among his readers. There are people who frankly say they cannot bear him, and then either honestly let him alone, or secretly hanker for him, and every now and then return to him, and try if they cannot like him, or cannot bear him a little better. These are his enemies, or may be called so for convenience' sake; but they are hardly to be considered his readers. Many of his readers, however, are also his enemies: they read him in a condition of hot insurrection against all that he says and is; they fiercely question his point of view, they object to the world that he sees from it; they declare that there is no such world, or that, if there is, there ought not to be, and that he does not paint it truly. They would like to have the question out with him personally: such is their difference of opinion that, to hear them talk, you would think they would like to have it out with him pugilistically. They would, to every appearance, like to beat also those who accept his point of view, believe in his world, and hold that he truly portrays it. Nothing but the prevailing sex of his enemies saves them, probably, from offering the readers who are not his enemies the violence to which their prevailing sex tempts them. You cannot, at least, palliate his demerits with them without becoming of the quality of his demerits, and identifying yourself with him in the whole measure of these. That is why, for one reason,

* *The North American Review* (January, 1903).

I am going to make my consideration of his later work almost entirely a study of his merits, for I own that he has his faults, and I would rather they remained his faults than became mine.

I

The enmity to Mr. James's fiction among his readers is mostly feminine because the men who do not like him are not his readers. The men who like him and are his readers are of a more feminine fineness, probably, in their perceptions and intuitions, than those other men who do not read him, though of quite as unquestionable a manliness, I hope. I should like to distinguish a little farther, and say that they are the sort of men whose opinions women peculiarly respect, and in whom they are interested quite as much as they are vexed to find them differing so absolutely from themselves.

The feminine enmity to Mr. James is of as old a date as his discovery of the Daisy Miller type of American girl, which gave continental offence among her sisters. It would be hard to say why that type gave such continental offence, unless it was because it was held not honestly to have set down the traits which no one could but most potently and powerfully allow to be true. The strange thing was that these traits were the charming and honorable distinctions of American girlhood as it convinced Europe, in the early eighteen-seventies, of a civilization so spiritual that its innocent daughters could be not only without the knowledge but without the fear of evil. I am not going back, however, to that early feminine grievance, except to note that it seems to have been the first tangible grievance, though it was not the first grievance. I, with my gray hairs, can remember still earlier work of his whose repugnant fascination was such that women readers clung to it with the wild rejection which has in a measure followed all his work at their hands.

It has been the curious fortune of this novelist, so supremely gifted in divining women and portraying them, that beyond any other great novelist (or little, for that matter) he has imagined few heroines acceptable to women. Even those martyr-women who have stood by him in the long course of his transgressions, and maintained through thick and thin, that he is by all odds the novelist whom they could best trust with the cause of woman in fiction, have liked his anti-heroines more,—I mean, found them realer,—than his heroines. I am not sure but I have liked them more myself, but that is because I always find larger play for my sympathies in the character which needs the reader's help than in that which is so perfect as to get on without it. If it were urged that women do not care for his heroines because there are none of them to care for, I should not blame them, still less should I blame him for giving them that ground for abhorrence. I find myself diffident of heroines in fiction because I have never known one in life, of the real faultless kind; and heaven forbid I should ever yet know one. In Mr. James's novels I always feel safe from that sort, and it may be for this reason, among others, that I like to read his novels when they are new, and read them over and over again when they are old, or when they are no longer recent.

II

At this point I hear from far within a voice bringing me to book about Milly Theale in *The Wings of a Dove*, asking me, if *there* is not a heroine of the ideal make, and demanding what fault there is in her that renders her lovable. Lovable, I allow she is, dearly, tenderly, reverently lovable, but she has enough to make her so, besides being too good, too pure, too generous, too magnificently unselfish. It is not imaginable that her author should have been conscious of offering in her anything like an atonement to the offended divinity of American womanhood for Daisy Miller. But if it were imaginable the offended divinity ought to be sumptuously appeased, appeased to tears of grateful pardon such as I have not yet seen in its eyes. Milly Theale is as entirely American in the qualities which you can and cannot touch as Daisy Miller herself; and (I find myself urged to the risk of noting it) she is largely American in the same things. There is the same self-regardlessness, the same beauteous insubordination, the same mortal solution of the problem. Of course, it is all in another region, and the social levels are immensely parted. Yet Milly Theale is the superior of Daisy Miller less in her nature than in her conditions.

There is, in both, the same sublime unconsciousness of the material environment, the same sovereign indifference to the fiscal means of their emancipation to a more than masculine independence. The sense of what money can do for an American girl without her knowing it, is a "blind sense" in the character of Daisy, but in the character of Milly it has its eyes wide open. In that wonderful way of Mr. James's by which he imparts a fact without stating it, approaching it again and again, without actually coming in contact with it, we are made aware of the vast background of wealth from which Milly is projected upon our acquaintance. She is shown in a kind of breathless impatience with it, except as it is the stuff of doing wilfully magnificent things, and committing colossal expenses without more anxiety than a prince might feel with the revenues of a kingdom behind him. The ideal American rich girl has never really been done before, and it is safe to say that she will never again be done with such exquisite appreciation. She is not of the new rich; an extinct New York ancestry darkles in the retrospect: something vaguely bourgeois, and yet with presences and with lineaments of aristocratic distinction. They have made her masses of money for her, those intangible fathers, uncles and grandfathers, and then, with her brothers and sisters, have all perished away from her, and left her alone in the world with nothing else. She is as convincingly imagined in her relation to them, as the daughter of an old New York family, as she is in her inherited riches. It is not the old New York family of the unfounded Knickerbocker tradition, but something as fully patrician, with a nimbus of social importance as unquestioned as its money. Milly is not so much the flower of this local root as something finer yet: the perfume of it, the distilled and wandering fragrance. It would be hard to say in what her New Yorkishness lies, and Mr. James himself by no means says; only if you know New York at all, you have the unmistakable sense of it. She is New Yorkish in the very essences that are least associable with the superficial notion of New York: the intellectual refinement that comes of being born and bred in conditions of illimitable ease, of having had everything that one could wish to have, and the cultivation that seems to come of the mere ability to command it. If one will have an illustration of the final effect in Milly Theale, it may be that it can be suggested as a sort of a Bostonian quality, with the element of *conscious* worth eliminated, and purified as essentially of pedantry as of commerciality. The wonder is that Mr. James in his prolonged expatriation has been able to seize this lovely impalpability, and to impart the sense of it; and perhaps the true reading of the riddle is that such a nature, such a character is most appreciable in that relief from the background which Europe gives all American character.

III

"But that is just what does not happen in the case of Mr. James's people. They are merged in the background so that you never can get behind them, and fairly feel and see them all round. Europe *doesn't* detach them; *nothing* does. 'There they are,' as he keeps making his people say in all his late books, when they are not calling one another dear lady, and dear man, and prodigious and magnificent, and of a vagueness or a richness, or a sympathy, or an opacity. No, he is of a tremendosity, but he worries me to death; he kills me; he really gives me a headache. He fascinates me, but I have no patience with him."

"But, dear lady," for it was a weary woman who had interrupted the flow of my censure in these unmeasured terms, and whom her interlocutor—another of Mr. James's insistent words—began trying to flatter to her disadvantage, "a person of your insight must see that this is the conditional vice of all painting, its vital fiction. You cannot get behind the figures in any picture. They are always merged in their background. And there you are!"

"Yes, I know I am. But that is just where I don't want to be. I want figures that I *can* get behind."

"Then you must go to some other shop—you must go to the shop of a sculptor."

"Well, why isn't *he* a sculptor?"

"Because he is a painter."

"Oh, that's no reason. He ought to be a sculptor."

"Then he couldn't give you the color, the light and shade, the delicate *nuances*, the joy of the intimated fact, all that you delight in him for. What was that you were saying the other day? That he was like Monticelli in some of his pastorals or picnics: a turmoil of presences which you could make anything, everything, nothing of as you happened to feel; something going on that you had glimpses of, or were allowed to guess at, but which you were rapturously dissatisfied with, any way."

"Did I say that?" my interlocutress—terrible word!—demanded. "It was very good."

"It was wonderfully good. I should not have named Monticelli, exactly, because though he is of a vagueness that is painty, he is too much of a denseness. Mr. James does not trowel the colors on."

"I see what you mean. Whom should you have named?"

"I don't know. Monticelli will do in one way. He gives you a sense of people, of things undeniably, though not unmistakably, happening, and that is what Mr. James does."

"Yes, he certainly does," and she sighed richly, as if she had been one of his people herself. "He does give you a sense."

"He gives you a sense of a tremendous lot going on, for instance, in *The Wings of a Dove,* of things undeniable, though not unmistakably, happening. It is a great book."

"It is, it is," she sighed again. "It wore me to a thread."

"And the people were as unmistakable as they were undeniable: not Milly, alone, not Mrs. Stringham, as wonderfully of New England as Milly of New York; but all that terribly frank, terribly selfish, terribly shameless, terribly hard English gang."

"Ah, Densher wasn't really hard or really shameless, though he was willing—to please that unspeakable Kate Croy—to make love to Milly and marry her money so that when she died, they could live happy ever after—or at least comfortably. And you cannot say that Kate was frank. And Lord Mark really admired Milly. Or, anyway, he wanted to marry her. Do you think Kate took the money from Densher at last and married Lord Mark?"

"Why should you care?"

"Oh, one oughtn't to care, of course, in reading Mr. James. But with any one else, you would like to know who married who. It is all too wretched. Why should he want to picture such life?"

"Perhaps because it exists."

"Oh, do you think the English are really so bad? I'm glad he made such a beautiful character as Milly, American."

"My notion is that he didn't 'make' any of the characters."

"Of course not. And I suppose some people in England are

actually like that. We have not got so far here, yet. To be sure, society is not so all-important here, yet. If it ever is, I suppose we shall pay the price. But *do* you think he ought to picture such life because it exists?"

"Do you find yourself much the worse for *The Wings of a Dove*?" I asked. "Or for *The Sacred Fount*? Or for *The Awkward Age*? Or even for *What Maisie Knew*? They all picture much the same sort of life."

"Why, of course not. But it isn't so much what he says—he never *says* anything—but what he insinuates. I don't believe that is good for young girls."

"But if they don't know what it means? I'll allow that it isn't quite *jeune fille* in its implications, all of them; but maturity has its modest claims. Even its immodest claims are not wholly ungrounded in the interest of a knowledge of our mother-civilization, which is what Mr. James's insinuations impart, as I understand them."

"Well, young people cannot read him aloud together. You can't deny that."

"No, but elderly people can, and they are not to be ignored by the novelist, always. I fancy the reader who brings some knowledge of good and evil, without being the worse for it, to his work is the sort of reader Mr. James writes for. I can imagine him addressing himself to a circle of such readers as this *Review's* with a satisfaction, and a sense of liberation, which he might not feel in the following of the family magazines, and still not incriminate himself. I have heard a good deal said in reproach of the sort of life he portrays, in his later books; but I have not found his people of darker deeds or murkier motives than the average in fiction. I don't say, life."

"No, certainly, so far as he tells you. It is what he *doesn't* tell that is so frightful. He leaves you to such awful conjectures. For instance when Kate Croy—"

"When Kate Croy—?"

"No. I *won't* discuss it. But you know what I mean; and I don't believe there ever was such a girl."

"And you believe there was ever such a girl as Milly Theale?"

"Hundreds! She is true to the life. So perfectly American. My husband and I read the story aloud together, and I wanted to weep. We had such a strange experience with that book. We read it half through together; then we got impatient, and tried to finish it alone. But we could not make anything of it apart; and we had to finish it together. We could not bear to lose a word; every word—and there were a good many!—seemed to tell. If you took one away you seemed to miss something important. It almost destroyed me, thinking it all out. I went round days, with my hand to my forehead; and I don't believe I understand it perfectly yet. Do you?"

IV

I pretended that I did, but I do not mind being honester with the reader than I was with my interlocutress. I have a theory that it is not well to penetrate every recess of an author's meaning. It robs him of the charm of mystery, and the somewhat labyrinthine construction of Mr. James's later sentences lends itself to the practice of the self-denial necessary to the preservation of this charm. What I feel sure of is that he has a meaning in it all, and that by and by, perhaps when I least expect it, I shall surprise his meaning. In the meanwhile I rest content with what I do know. In spite of all the Browning Clubs —even the club which has put up a monument to the poet's butler-ancestor—all of Browning is not clear, but enough of Browning is clear for any real lover of his poetry.

I was sorry I had not thought of this in time to say it to my interlocutress; and I was sorry I had not amplified what I did say of his giving you a sense of things, so as to make it apply to places as well as persons. Never, in my ignorance, have I had a vivider sense of London, in my knowledge a stronger sense of Venice, than in *The Wings of a Dove*. More miraculous still, as I have tried to express, was the sense he gave me of the anterior New York where the life flowered which breathed out the odor called Milly Theale—a heartbreaking fragance as of funeral violets—and of the anterior New England sub-acidly fruiting in Mrs. Stringham. As for social conditions, predicaments, orders of things, where shall we find the like of the wonders wrought in *The Awkward Age?* I have been trying to get phrases which should convey the effect of that psychomancy from me to my reader, and I find none so apt as some phrase that should suggest the convincingly incredible. Here is something that the reason can as little refuse as it can accept. Into quite such particles as the various characters of this story would the disintegration of the old, rich, demoralized society of an ancient capital fall so probably that each of the kaleidoscopic fragments, dropping into irrelevant radiance around Mrs. Brookenham, would have its fatally appointed tone in the "scheme of color." Here is that inevitable, which Mr. Brander Matthews has noted as the right and infallible token of the real. It does not matter, after that, how the people talk,—or in what labyrinthine parentheses they let their unarriving language wander. They strongly and vividly exist, and they construct not a drama, perhaps, but a world, floating indeed in an obscure where it seems to have its solitary orbit, but to be as solidly palpable as any of the planets of the more familiar systems, and wrapt in the aura of its peculiar corruption. How bad the bad people on it may be, one does not know, and is not intended to know, perhaps; that would be like being told the gross facts of some scandal which, so long as it was untouched, supported itself not unamusingly in air; but of the goodness of the good people one is not left in doubt; and it is a goodness which consoles and sustains the virtue apt to droop in the presence of neighborly remissness.

I might easily attribute to the goodness a higher office than this; but if I did I might be trenching upon that ethical delicacy of the author which seems to claim so little for itself. Mr. James is, above any other, the master of the difficult art of never doing more than to "hint a fault, or hesitate dislike," and I am not going to try committing him to conclusions he would shrink from. There is nothing of the clumsiness of the "satirist" in his design, and if he notes the absolute commerciality of the modern London world, it is with a reserve clothing itself in frankness which is infinitely, as he would say, "detached." But somehow, he lets you know how horribly *business* fashionable English life is; he lets Lord Mark let Milly Theale know, at their first meeting, when he tells her she is with people who never do anything for nothing, and when, with all her money, and perhaps because of it, she is still so trammelled in the ideal that she cannot take his meaning. Money, and money bluntly; gate-money of all kinds; money the means, is the tune to which that old world turns in a way which we scarcely imagine in this crude new world where it is still so largely less the means than the end.

But the general is lost in the personal, as it should be in Mr. James's books, earlier as well as later, and the allegory is so faint that it cannot always be traced. He does not say that the limitless liberty allowed Nanda Brookenham by her mother in *The Awkward Age* is better than the silken bondage in which the Duchess keeps her niece Aggie, though Nanda is admirably lovable, and little Aggie is a little cat; that is no more his affair than to insist upon the loyalty of old Mr. Longdon to an early love, or the generosity of Mitchett, as contrasted with the rapacity of Mrs. Brookenham, who, after all, wants nothing more than the means of being what she has always been. What he does is simply to show you those people mainly on the outside, as you mainly see people in the world, and to let you divine them and their ends from what they do and say. They are presented with infinite pains; as far as their appearance (though they are very little described) goes, you are not suffered to make a mistake. But he does not analyze them for you; rather he synthetizes them, and carefully hands them over to you in a sort of integrity very uncommon in the characters of fiction. One might infer from this that his method was dramatic, something like Tourguénieff's, say; but I do not know that his method is dramatic. I do not recall from the book more than one passage of dramatic intensity, but that was for me of very great intensity; I mean the passage where old Mr. Longdon lets Vanderbank understand that he will provide for him if he will offer himself to Nanda, whom he knows to be in love with Vanderbank, and where Vanderbank will not promise. That is a great moment, where everything is most openly said, most brutally said, to American thinking; and yet said with a restraint of feeling that somehow redeems it all.

Nothing could well be more perfected than the method of the three books which I have been supposing myself to be talking about, however far any one may think it from perfect. They express mastery, finality, doing what one means, in a measure not easily to be matched. I will leave out of the question the question of obscurity; I will let those debate that whom it interests more than it interests me. For my own part I take it that a master of Mr. James's quality does not set out with a design whose significance is not clear to himself, and if others do not make it clear to themselves, I suspect them rather than him of the fault. All the same I allow that it is sometimes not easy to make out; I allow that sometimes *I* do not make it out, I, who delight to read him almost more than any other living author, but then I leave myself in his hands. I do not believe he is going finally to play me the shabby trick of abandoning me in the dark; and meanwhile he perpetually interests me. If anything, he interests me too much, and I come away fatigued, because I cannot bear to lose the least pulse of the play of character; whereas from most fiction I lapse into long delicious absences of mind, now and then comfortably recovering myself to find out what is going on, and then sinking below the surface again.

The Awkward Age is mostly expressed in dialogue; *The Wings of a Dove* is mostly in the narration and the synthesis of emotions. Not the synthesis of the motives, please; these in both books are left to the reader, almost as much as they are in *The Sacred Fount*. That troubled source, I will own, "is of a profundity," and in its depths darkles the solution which the author makes it no part of his business to pull to the top; if the reader wants it, let him dive. But why should not a novel be written so like to life, in which most of the events remain the meaningless, that we shall never quite know what the author meant? Why, in fact, should not people come and go, and love and hate, and hurt and help one another as they do in reality, without rendering the reader a reason for their behavior, or offering an explanation at the end with which he can light himself back over the way he has come, and see what they meant? Who knows what any one means here below, or what he means himself, that is, precisely stands for? Most people mean nothing, except from moment to moment, if they indeed mean anything so long as that, and life which is full of propensities is almost without motives. In the scribbles which we suppose to be imitations of life, we hold the unhappy author to a logical consistency which we find so rarely in the original; but ought not we rather to praise him where his work confesses itself, as life confesses itself, without a plan? Why should we demand more of the imitator than we get from the creator?

Of course, it can be answered that we are *in* creation like characters in fiction, while we are outside of the imitation and spectators instead of characters; but that does not wholly cover the point. Perhaps, however, I am asking more for Mr. James than he would have me. In that case I am willing to offer him the reparation of a little detraction. I wish he would leave his people more, not less, to me when I read him. I have tried following their speeches without taking in his comment, delightfully pictorial as that always is, and it seems to me that I make rather more of their meaning, that way. I reserve the pleasure and privilege of going back and reading his comment in the light of my conclusions. This is the method I have largely pursued with the people of *The Sacred Fount*, of which I do not hestitate to say that I have mastered the secret, though, for the present I am not going to divulge it. Those who cannot wait may try the key which I have given.

But do not, I should urge them, expect too much of it; I do not promise it will unlock everything. If you find yourself, at the end, with nothing in your hand but the postulate with which the supposed narrator fantastically started, namely, that people may involuntarily and unconsciously prey upon one another, and mentally and psychically enrich themselves at one another's expense, still you may console yourself, if you do not think this enough, with the fact that you have passed the time in the company of men and women freshly and truly seen, amusingly shown, and abidingly left with your imagination. For me, I am so little exacting, that this is enough.

The Sacred Fount is a most interesting book, and you are teased through it to the end with delightful skill, but I am not going to say that it is a great book like *The Awkward Age*, or *The Wings of a Dove*. These are really incomparable books, not so much because there is nothing in contemporary fiction to equal them as because there is nothing the least like them. They are of a kind that none but their author can do, and since he is alone master of their art, I am very well content to leave him to do that kind of book quite as he chooses. I will not so abandon my function as to say that I could not tell him how to do them better, but it sufficiently interests me to see how he gets on without my help. After all, the critic has to leave authors somewhat to themselves; he cannot always be writing their books for them; and when I find an author, like Mr. James, who makes me acquainted with people who instantly pique my curiosity by "something rich and strange," in an environment which is admirably imaginable, I gratefully make myself at home with them, and stay as long as he will let me.

V

"But,"—here is that interlocutress whom I flattered myself I had silenced, at me again,—"do you like to keep puzzling things out, so? I don't. Of course, the books *are* intensely fascinating, but I do not like to keep guessing conundrums. Why shouldn't we have studies of life that are not a series of conundrums?"

"Dear lady," I make my answer, "what was I saying just now but that life itself is a series of conundrums, to which the answers are lost in the past, or are to be supplied us, after a long and purifying discipline of guessing, in the future? I do not admit your position, but if I did, still I should read the author who keeps you guessing, with a pleasure, an edification, in the suggestive, the instructive way he has of asking his conundrums beyond that I take in any of the authors who do not tax my curiosity, who shove their answers at me before I have had a chance to try whether I cannot guess them. Here you have the work of a great psychologist, who has the imagination of a poet, the wit of a keen humorist, the conscience of an impeccable moralist, the temperament of a philosopher, and the wisdom of a rarely experienced witness of the world; and yet you come back at me with the fact, or rather the pretence, that you do not like to keep puzzling his things out. It is my high opinion of you that you precisely do like to keep puzzling his things out; that you are pleased with the sort of personal appeal made to you by the difficulties you pretend to resent, and that you enjoy the just sense of superiority which your continual or final divinations give you. Mr. James is one of those authors who pay the finest tribute an author can pay the intelligence of his reader by trusting it, fully and frankly. There you are; and if you were not puzzling out those recondite conundrums which you complain of, what better things, in the perusal of the whole range of contemporary fiction, could you be doing? For my part I can think for you of none. There is no book like *The Awkward Age,* as I said, for it is sole of its kind, and no book that at all equals it, since Mr. Hardy's *Jude,* for the intensity of its naturalness. I don't name them to compare them; again I renounce all comparisons for Mr. James's work; but I will say that in the deeply penetrating anguish of *Jude,* I felt nothing profounder than the pathos which aches and pierces through those closing scenes of *The Awkward Age,* in Nanda's last talk with Vanderbank, whom she must and does have for her mother's amusement, and her yet later talk with old Mr. Longdon, to whom she must and does own her love for Vanderbank so heartbreaking. What beautiful and gentle souls the new-fashioned young girl and the old-fashioned old man are, and how beautifully and gently they are revealed to us by the perfected art of the book in which they continue to live after we part with them! How—"

"Ah, there," my interlocutress broke in, as if fearful of not having the last word. "I certainly agree with you. I wish you were as candid about everything else."